STABLE TO TH

by

Maralyn B. Dyck
[Combined Gospels]

Assistant Editor
Peter H. Dyck

Cover Photo by Patricia R. Miller

This book belongs to:________________________________

First printing: June 1996
Second edition: November 2015
This edition: May 2016

DISCLAIMER STATEMENT

The four New Testament Gospels are independent books in the Bible, each witnessing from its own perspective to the life, work, message and meaning of Jesus Christ. In this book passages from each of these four Gospels have been edited and combined into one continuous narrative with only the duplications eliminated.

All arrangements involved in combining the four Gospels are entirely the responsibility of the author.

Walk Where Jesus Walked

Hear again the voice of one "shouting in the desert" as John the Baptist points out the One who is the Lamb of God, He who has come to take away the sin of the world.

Hear young Mary as she worships God because she believed the supernatural messenger.

Walk with the One of whom the prophet said that he would "bring fathers and children together again."

See Jesus, the man from Galilee, identify with the poor as he feeds the hungry, heals the crippled and brings to life the dead.

Feel the peace after the storm, and they exclaim, "...even the wind and the waves obey him!"

Then as the few short years go by we must inevitably follow him to the lonely hill of Golgotha and through tears declare our faith with the army officer and soldiers; "He really was the Son of God!"

They had great plans, but now, was it the end?

Follow Mary and the other women early on Sunday morning to the tomb.

Listen to unbelievable words of hope: "He is not here; he has been raised."

About 40 days later with renewed faith we follow him out of the city of Jerusalem and watch him ascend up into heaven with the angels' assurance, "This Jesus ... will come back!"

Peter H. Dyck

PREFACE

Matthew, Mark, Luke and John have been carefully interwoven into one continuous story. All the events and teachings were placed into chronological order with the duplications edited out.

For *Stable to Throne* the book of Mark has been used as the "pilot" book, since harmonists consider his writing to be the most accurate chronological order.

SQUARE BRACKETS enclose comments by the Editor.

ROUND BRACKETS are part of the scriptures.

INSIGHT BOXES provide further information and facts of special interest, including the journeys of Jesus

FP identifies a major fulfilled prophecy when placed beside a scripture reference.

Editor's Note: This book is not intended to be used as a replacement for the four gospels. Stable to Throne is intended to be used as a tool to spread the Good News of Jesus Christ and introduce the readers to the wonders to be found in the complete Holy Bible. I recommend that the reader buy a New Testament or complete Holy Bible to discover all the truths that God has provided for His people.

Numbering: The numbered sections throughout the book are to help you when using the book as a daily reading or study guide.

Scripture references: Provide the scriptures used for combining each section. This makes it easier for leaders to prepare sermons and articles, giving them a quick reference to the actual locations in the four gospels for study purposes.

Table of Contents

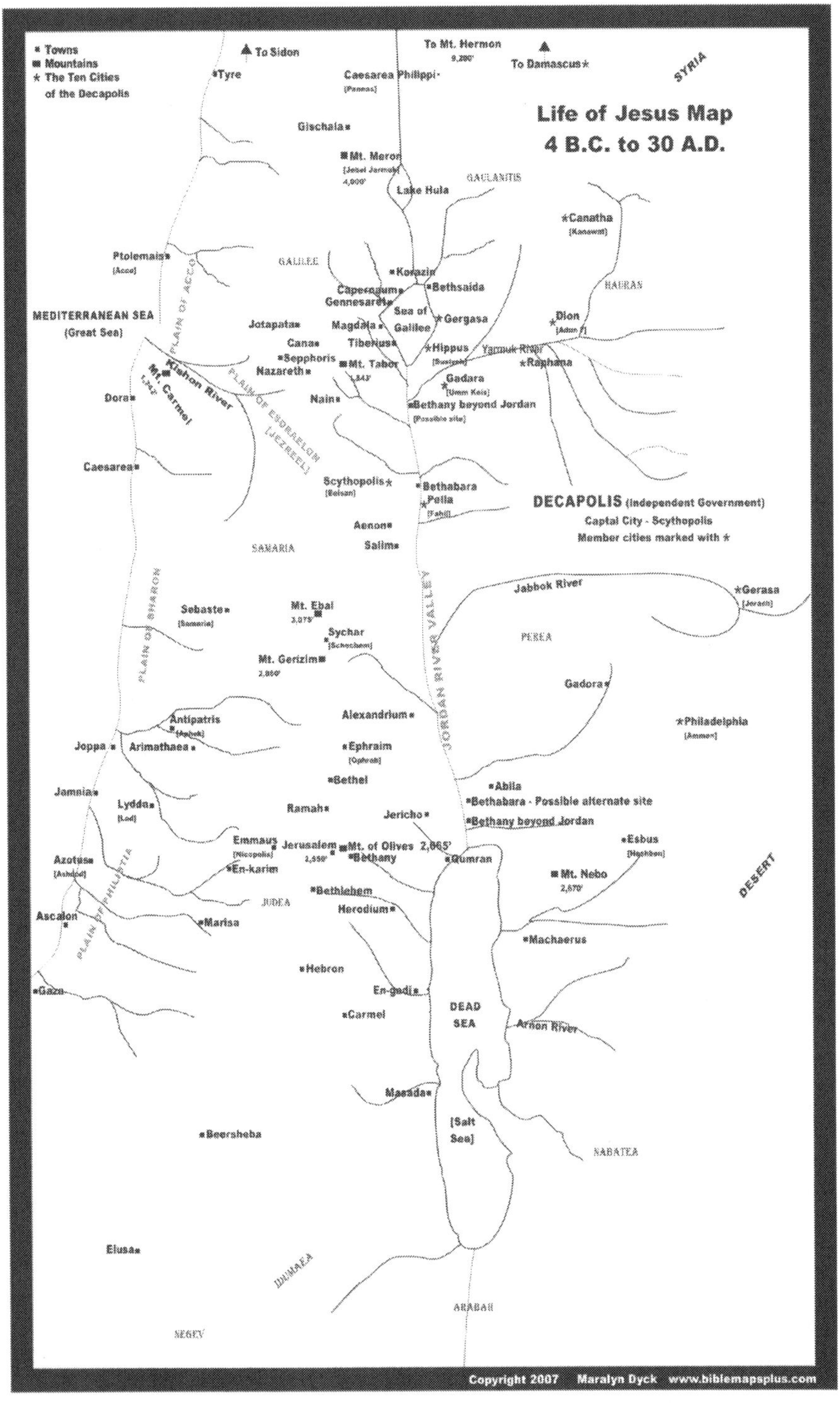

Towns
Mountains
The Ten Cities of the Decapolis
To Sidon
Tyre
To Mt. Hermon
9,280'
To Damascus
SYRIA
Caesarea Philippi
(Paneas)
Life of Jesus Map
4 B.C. to 30 A.D.
Gischala
Mt. Meron
4,000'
GAULANITIS
Lake Hula
Canatha
(Kanawat)
Ptolemais
(Acco)
GALILEE
PLAIN OF ACCO
Korazin
Bethsaida
Capernaum
Gennesaret
HAURAN
Sea of Galilee
MEDITERRANEAN SEA
(Great Sea)
Jotapata
Magdala
Gergasa
Dion
Cana
Tiberius
Hippus
Yarmuk River
Raphana
Sepphoris
Nazareth
Mt. Tabor
1,843'
Kishon River
Mt. Carmel
Gadara
(Umm Keis)
Dora
PLAIN OF ESDRAELON
(JEZREEL)
Nain
Bethany beyond Jordan
(Possible site)
Caesarea
Scythopolis
(Beisan)
Bethabara
Pella
(Fahil)
DECAPOLIS (Independent Government)
Captal City - Scythopolis
Member cities marked with ★
Aenon
SAMARIA
Salim
JORDAN RIVER VALLEY
Jabbok River
Gerasa
(Jerash)
Sebaste
(Samaria)
Mt. Ebal
3,075'
PLAIN OF SHARON
Sychar
(Schechem)
PEREA
Mt. Gerizim
2,850'
Gadora
Antipatris
(Aphek)
Alexandrium
Philadelphia
(Ammon)
Joppa
Arimathaea
Ephraim
(Ophrah)
Bethel
Jamnia
Abila
Bethabara - Possible alternate site
Lydda
(Lod)
Ramah
Jericho
Bethany beyond Jordan
Emmaus
(Nicopolis)
Jerusalem
2,550'
Mt. of Olives 2,665'
Bethany
Qumran
Esbus
(Heshbon)
Azotus
(Ashdod)
En-karim
Mt. Nebo
2,670'
DESERT
PLAIN OF PHILISTIA
JUDEA
Bethlehem
Herodium
Ascalon
Marisa
Machaerus
Hebron
Gaza
En-gedi
DEAD SEA
Carmel
Arnon River
Masada
(Salt Sea)
Beersheba
NABATEA
Elusa
IDUMAEA
ARABAH
NEGEV
Copyright 2007 Maralyn Dyck www.biblemapsplus.com

I. JESUS' EARLY YEARS

The period from Jesus' birth to his baptism covers thirty years and involves four journeys.

Introduction

Mark 1:1; Luke 1:1-4

Many people have tried to tell the story of what God has done among us. They wrote what we had been told by the ones who were there in the beginning and saw what happened.

And so, I made a careful study of everything and then decided to write and tell you exactly what took place. Honorable Theophilus, I have done this to let you will know the truth about what you have heard.

This is the Good News about Jesus Christ, the Son of God.

1 The Word of Life

John 1:1-18

In the beginning was the one who is called the Word. The Word was with God, God created all things. Nothing was made without the Word. Everything that was created received its life from Him, and His light gave life to everyone. The light keeps shining in the dark, and darkness has never put it out.

God sent a man named John, who came to tell about the light and to lead all people to have faith. John wasn't that light, he came only to tell about the light. The true light that shines on everyone was coming into the world. The Word was in the world, but no one knew Him, though God had made the world with His Word.

He came into his own world, but His own nation did not welcome him. Yet some people accepted Him and put their faith in Him, so He gave them the right to become the children of God. They were not God's children by nature or because of any human desires. God himself was the one who made them His children.

The Word became a human being [Jesus] and lived here with us. We saw His true glory, the glory of the only Son of the Father. From Him all the kindness and all the truth of God have come down to us.

John spoke about Him and shouted, "This is the one I told you would come! He is greater than I am because He was alive before I was born."

Because of all that the Son is, we have been given one blessing after another.

The law was given by Moses, but Jesus Christ brought us undeserved kindness and truth. No one has ever seen God.

The only Son, who is truly God and is closest to the father, has shown what God is like.

2 Ancestors of Jesus Christ

Matthew 1:1-17; Luke 3:23-38

Jesus Christ came from the family of King David and also from the family of Abraham. And this is a list of his ancestors. From Abraham to King David, his ancestors were:

[Matthew] **Abraham**, **Isaac**, **Jacob**, **Judah** and his brothers (Judah's sons were Perez and Zerah and their mother was Tamar), Hezron;

Ram, Ammindab, Nahshon, Salmon, **Boaz** (his mother was Rahab), **Obed** (his mother was Ruth), **Jesse,** and **King David.**

From David to the time of the exile in Babylonia, the ancestors of Jesus were: David, **Solomon** (his mother had been Uriah's wife), Rehoboam, Abijah, Asa, Jehoshaphat, Jehoram;

Uzziah, Jotham, Ahaz, Hezekiah, Manasseh, Amon, Josiah, and Jehoiachin and his brothers.

From the exile to the birth of Jesus, his ancestors were:

Jehoiachin, Shealtiel, Zerubbabel, Abiud, Eliakim, Azor, Zadok, Achim; Eliud, Eleazar, Matthan, Jacob, and **Joseph,** the husband of **Mary,** the mother of **Jesus,** who is called the Messiah.

There were fourteen generations from Abraham to David. There were also fourteen from David to the exile in Babylonia and fourteen more to the birth of the Messiah.

Insight: *Some historians believe the genealogy in Matthew is Joseph's blood line while the genealogy in Luke is Mary's blood line, Heli being Mary's father. Both were descendants of King David, Joseph through Solomon and Mary through Nathan. [Solomon and Nathan were brothers.] [Luke 3]*

When Jesus began to preach, he was about thirty years old. Everyone thought he was the son of Joseph.

But his family went back through Heli, Matthat, Levi, Melchi, Jannai, Joseph, Mattathias, Amos, Nahum, Esli, Naggai, Maath, Mattathias, Semein, Josech, Joda; Joanan, Rhesa, Zerubbabel, Shealtiel, Neri, Melchi, Addi, Cosam, Elmadam, Er, Joshua, Eliezer, Jorim, Matthat, Levi; Simeon, Judah, Joseph, Jonam, Eliakim, Melea, Menna, Mattatha, **Nathan, David, Jesse, Obed, Boaz,** Salmon, Nahshon; Ammindab, Admin, Arni, Hezron, Perez, **Judah, Jacob, Isaac, Abraham, Terah,** Nahor, Serug, Reu, Peleg, Eber, Shelah;Cainan, Arphaxad, **Shem, Noah, Lamech, Methuselah, Enoch,** Jared, Mahalaleel, Kenan, Enosh and **Seth.**

The family of Jesus went all the way back to **Adam** and then to **God.**

3 John's Birth Announced

Luke 1:5-25

During the time when Herod was king of Judea, there was a priest named Zechariah, who belonged to the priestly order of Abijah. His wife's name was Elizabeth; she also belonged to a priestly family. They both lived good lives in God's sight and obeyed fully all the Lord's laws and commands.

They had no children because Elizabeth could not have any, and she and Zechariah were both very old. One day Zechariah was doing his work as a priest in the Temple, taking his turn in the daily service. According to the custom followed by the priests, he was chosen by lot to burn incense on the altar. So he went into the Temple of the Lord, while the crowd of people outside prayed during the hour when the incense was burned. An angel of the Lord appeared to him, standing at the right side of the altar where the incense was burned. When Zechariah saw him, he was alarmed and felt afraid.

But the angel said to him, "Don't be afraid, Zechariah! God has heard your prayer, and your wife Elizabeth will bear you a son. You are to name him John.

How glad and happy you will be, and how happy many others will be when he is born! John will be great in the Lord's sight. He must not drink any wine or strong drink. From his very birth he will be filled with the Holy Spirit, and he will bring back many of the people of Israel to the Lord their God.

He will go ahead of the Lord, strong and mighty like the prophet Elijah. He will bring fathers and children together again; he will turn disobedient people back to the way of thinking of the righteous; he will get the Lord's people ready for Him."

Zechariah said to the angel, "How shall I know if this is so? I am an old man and my wife is old also."

"I am Gabriel," the angel answered. "I stand in the presence of God, who sent me to speak to you and tell you this good news. But you have not believed my message, which will come true at the right time. Because you have not believed, you will be unable to speak; you will remain silent until the day my promise to you comes true."

In the meantime the people were waiting for Zechariah and wondering why he was spending such a long time in the Temple. When he came out, he could not speak to them, and so they knew that he had seen a vision in the Temple. Unable to say a word, he made signs to them with his hands.

When his period of service in the Temple was over, Zechariah went back home.

Sometime later his wife Elizabeth became pregnant and did not leave the house for five months.

"Now at last the Lord has helped me," she said. "He has taken away my public disgrace!"

4 Jesus' Birth Announced

Luke 1:26-38

In the sixth month of Elizabeth's pregnancy God sent the angel Gabriel to a town in Galilee named Nazareth. He had a message for a young woman promised in marriage to a man named Joseph, who was a descendant of King David. Her name was Mary. The angel came to her and said, "Peace be with you! The Lord is with you and has greatly blessed you!"

Mary was deeply troubled by the angel's message, and she wondered what his words meant. The angel said to her, "Don't be afraid, Mary; God has been gracious to you. You will become pregnant and give birth to a son, and you will name him Jesus. He will be great and will be called the Son of the Most High God. The Lord God will make Him a king, as His ancestor David was, and He will be the king of the descendants of Jacob forever; His kingdom will never end!"

Mary said to the angel, "I am a virgin. How, then, can this be?"

The angel answered, "The Holy Spirit will come on you, and God's power will rest upon you. For this reason the holy child will be called the Son of God. Remember your relative Elizabeth. It is said that she cannot have children, but she herself is now six months pregnant, even though she is very old. For there is nothing that God cannot do."

"I am the Lord's servant," said Mary; "may it happen to me as you have said." And the angel left her.

5 Mary Visits Elizabeth

Luke 1:39-45

Soon afterward Mary got ready and hurried off to a town in the hill country of Judea. She went into Zechariah's house and greeted Elizabeth. When Elizabeth heard Mary's greeting, the baby moved within her. Elizabeth was filled with the Holy Spirit, and said in a loud voice, "You are the most blessed of all women, and blessed is the child you will bear!

Why should this great thing happen to me, that my Lord's mother comes to visit me? For as soon as I heard your greeting, the baby within me jumped with gladness. How happy are you to believe that the Lord's message to you will come true!"

6 Mary's Song of Praise

Luke 1:46-56

Mary said,

"My heart praises the Lord; my soul is glad
because of God my Savior,
for he has remembered me, his lowly servant!
From now on all people will call me happy,
because of the great things the Mighty God has done for me.

His name is holy;
from one generation to another
he shows mercy to those who honor him.

He has stretched out his mighty arm
and scattered the proud with all their plans.

He has brought down mighty kings from their thrones,
He has filled the hungry with good things,
and sent the rich away with empty hands.

He has kept the promise he made to our ancestors,
and has come to the help of his servant Israel.

He has remembered to show mercy to Abraham and to all his
descendants forever!"

Mary stayed about three months with Elizabeth and then went back home.

7 Birth of John the Baptist

Luke 1:57-66

The time came for Elizabeth to have her baby, and she gave birth to a son. Her neighbors and relatives heard how wonderfully good the Lord had been to her, and they all rejoiced with her.

When the baby was a week old, they came to circumcise him, and they were going to name him Zechariah, after his father. But his mother said, "No! His name is to be John." They said to her, "But you don't have any relative with that name!"

Then they made signs to his father, asking him what name he would like the boy to have. Zechariah asked for a writing pad and wrote, "His name is John." How surprised they all were! At that moment Zechariah was able to speak again, and he started praising God.

The neighbors were all filled with fear, and the news about these things spread through all the hill country of Judea. Everyone who heard of it thought about it and asked, "What is this child going to be?" For it was plain that the Lord's power was upon him.

8 Zechariah's Prophecy

Luke 1:67-80

John's father Zechariah was filled with the Holy Spirit, and he spoke God's message.

"Let us praise the Lord, the God of Israel! He has come to
the help of His people and has set them free.

He has provided for us a mighty Savior,
a descendant of his servant David.

He promised through His holy prophets long ago
that he would save us from our enemies,
from the power of all those who hate us.

He said He would show mercy to our ancestors
and remember His sacred covenant.

With a solemn oath to our ancestor Abraham
He promised to rescue us from our enemies
and allow us to serve Him without fear,
so that we might be holy and righteous before Him
all the days of our life.

"You, my child, will be called a prophet of
the Most High God.
"You will go ahead of the Lord to prepare His road for Him,
to tell His people that they will be saved by having their sins forgiven.

"Our God is merciful and tender.

"He will cause the bright dawn of salvation to rise on us
and to shine from heaven on all those
who live in the dark shadow of death,
to guide our steps into the path of peace."

The child grew and developed in body and spirit. He lived in the desert until the day when he appeared publicly to the people of Israel.

9 Birth of Jesus

Matthew 1:18-25a; Mark 1:1; Luke 2:1-7

This was how the birth of Jesus Christ took place. His mother Mary was engaged to Joseph, but before they were married, she found out that she was going to have a baby by the Holy Spirit. Joseph was a man who always did what was right, but he did not want to disgrace Mary publicly; so he made plans to break the engagement privately.

While he was thinking about this, an angel of the Lord appeared to him in a dream and said, "Joseph, descendant of David, do not be afraid to take Mary to be your wife. For it is by the Holy Spirit that she has conceived. She will have a son, and you will name him Jesus because He will save His people from their sins."

Now all this happened in order to make come true what the Lord had said through the prophet, "A virgin will become pregnant and have a son, and He will be called Immanuel" (which means, "God is with us"). FP Isaiah 7:14

So when Joseph woke up, he married Mary, as the angel of the Lord had told him to.

But he had no sexual relations with her before she gave birth to her son.

At that time Emperor Augustus ordered a census to be taken throughout the Roman Empire.

When this first census took place, Quirinius was the governor of Syria. Everyone, then, went to register himself, each to his own hometown.

Joseph went from the town of Nazareth in Galilee to the town of Bethlehem in Judea, the birthplace of King David.

Joseph went there because he was a descendant of David.

He went to register with Mary, who was promised in marriage to him. She was pregnant, and while they were in Bethlehem, the time came for her to have her baby. She gave birth to her first son, wrapped him in cloths and laid him in a manger—there was no room for them to stay in the inn.

10 Shepherds and the Angels

Luke 2:8-20

There were some shepherds in that part of the country who were spending the night in the fields, taking care of their flocks. An angel of the Lord appeared to them, and the glory of the Lord shone over them. They were terribly afraid, but the angel said to them, "Don't be afraid! I am here with good news for you, which will bring great joy to all the people. This very day in David's town your Savior was born—Christ the Lord! And this is what will prove it to you: you will find a baby wrapped in cloths and lying in a manger."

Suddenly a great army of heaven's angels appeared with the angel, singing praises to God:

"Glory to God in the highest heaven, and peace on earth to those with whom He is pleased!"

When the angels went away from them back into heaven, the shepherds said to one another, "Let's go to Bethlehem and see this thing that has happened, which the Lord has told us." So they hurried off and found Mary and Joseph and saw the baby lying in the manger. When the shepherds saw Him, they told them what the angel had said about the child. All who heard it were amazed at what the shepherds said. Mary remembered all these things and thought deeply about them. The shepherds went back, singing praises to God for all they had heard and seen; it had been just as the angel had told them.

11 Jesus is Named

Matthew 1;25b; Luke 2:21

A week later, when the time came for the baby to be circumcised, he was named Jesus, the name which the angel had given him before he had been conceived.

12 Jesus Presented in the Temple

Luke 2:22-38

The time came for Mary and Joseph to do what the law of Moses says a mother is supposed to do after her baby is born. They took Jesus to the temple in Jerusalem and presented him to the Lord, just as the law of the Lord says," Each first-born baby boy belongs to the Lord."

Insight: *The Ceremony of Purification took place when Jesus was forty days old.*

The Law of the Lord also says that parents have to offer a sacrifice, giving at least a pair of doves or two young pigeons. So that is what Mary and Joseph did.

Insight: *First journey: From Bethlehem to Jerusalem and return.*

At this time a man named Simeon was living in Jerusalem. Simeon was a good man. He loved God and was waiting for God to save the people of Israel. God's Spirit came to him and told him that he would not die until he had seen Christ the Lord. When Mary and Joseph brought Jesus to do what the Law of Moses says should be done for a new baby, the Spirit told Simeon to go into the temple. Simeon took the baby Jesus in his arms and praised God:

"Lord, I am your servant, and now I can die in peace.
because you have kept your promise to me.

"With my own eyes I have seen what you have done
to save your people, and foreign nations will also see this.
Your mighty power is a light for all nations and it will
bring honor to your people Israel."

Jesus' parents were surprised at what Simeon had said. Then he blessed them and told Mary, "This child of yours will cause many people in Israel to fall and others to stand. The child will be like a warning sign. Many people will reject him, and you, Mary, will suffer as though you had been stabbed by a dagger. But all this will show what people are really thinking."

There was a very old prophetess, a widow named Anna, daughter of Phanuel, of the tribe of Asher. She had been married for only seven years and was now eighty-four years old.

Night and day she served God in the temple by praying and often going without eating. At that time Anna came in and praised God. She spoke about the child Jesus to everyone who hoped for Jerusalem to be set free.

13 Visitors from the East

Matthew 2:1-12

Jesus was born in the town of Bethlehem in Judea, during the time when Herod was king. Soon afterward, some men who studied the stars came from the East to Jerusalem and asked, "Where is the baby born to be the king of the Jews?

We saw his star when it came up in the east, and we have come to worship him."

When King Herod heard about this, he was very upset, and so was everyone else in Jerusalem. He called together all the chief priests and the teachers of the Law and asked them, "Where will the Messiah be born?"

"In the town of Bethlehem in Judea," they answered. "For this is what the prophet wrote:

'Bethlehem, in the land of Judah, you are by
no means the least of the leading cities of Judah;
for from you will come a leader
who will guide my people Israel.'" FP Micah 5:2

So Herod called the visitors from the East to a secret meeting and found out from them the exact time the star had appeared.

Then he sent them to Bethlehem with these instructions: "Go and make a careful search for the child; and when you find him let me know, so that I too may go and worship him."

And so they left, and on their way they saw the same star they had seen in the East.

When they saw it, how happy they were, what joy was theirs! It went ahead of them until it stopped over the place where the child was.

They went into the house, and when they saw the child with his mother Mary, they knelt down and worshiped him. They brought out their gifts of gold, frankincense, and myrrh, and presented them to him.

Then they returned to their country by another road, since God had warned them in a dream not to go back to Herod.

Insight: *Second journey—From Bethlehem to Egypt where he remained until Herod's death.*

14 Escape to Egypt

Matthew 2:13-15

After they had left, an angel of the Lord appeared in a dream to Joseph and said, "Herod will be looking for the child in order to kill him.

So get up, take the child and his mother and escape to Egypt, and stay there until I tell you to leave."

Joseph got up, took the child and his mother, and left during the night for Egypt, where he stayed until Herod died. This was done to make come true what the Lord had said through the prophet, "I called my Son out of Egypt." FP Hosea 11:1

15 Killing of the Children

Matthew 2:16-18

When Herod realized that the visitors from the east had tricked him, he was furious. He gave orders to kill all the boys in Bethlehem and its neighborhood who were two years old and younger. This was done in accordance with what he had learned from the visitors about the time when the star had appeared. In this way what the prophet Jeremiah had said came true:

"A sound is heard in Ramah,
the sound of bitter weeping.
Rachel is crying for her children;
she refuses to be comforted,
for they are dead." FP Jeremiah 31:15

16 Return from Egypt

Matthew 2:19-21

After Herod had died, an angel of the Lord appeared in a dream to Joseph in Egypt and said, "Get up, take the child and his mother, and go back to the land of Israel, because those who tried to kill the child are dead."

Insight: *Third journey—From Egypt to Nazareth.*

So Joseph got up, took the child and his mother, and went back to Israel.

17 Return to Nazareth

Matthew 2:22-23; Luke 2:39-40

But when Joseph heard that Archelaus had succeeded his father Herod as king of Judea, he was afraid to go there. He was given more instructions in a dream, so he went to the province of Galilee and made his home in a town named Nazareth. And so what the prophets had said came true; "He will be called a Nazarene." FP

The child grew and became strong; he was full of wisdom, and God's blessings were upon him.

18 Jesus in the Temple

Luke 2:41-52

Every year the parents of Jesus went to Jerusalem for the Passover Festival.

When Jesus was twelve years old, they went to the festival as usual.

When the festival was over, they started back home, but the boy Jesus stayed in Jerusalem. His parents did not know this; they thought that he was with the group, so they traveled a whole day and then started looking for him among their relatives and friends.

They did not find him, so they went back to Jerusalem looking for him. On the third day they found him in the Temple, sitting with the Jewish teachers, listening to them and asking questions. All who heard him were amazed at his intelligent answers. His parents were astonished when they saw him, and his mother said to him, "Son, why have you done this to us? Your father and I have been terribly worried trying to find you."

He answered them, "Why did you have to look for me? Didn't you know that I had to be in my Father's house?"

But they did not understand his answer.

So Jesus went back with them to Nazareth, where he was obedient to them. His mother treasured all these things in her heart. Jesus grew both in body and in wisdom, gaining favor with God and people.

II. JESUS BEGINS HIS MINISTRY

The time of inauguration, a period of 15 months, covers the period from Jesus' baptism to his rejection at Nazareth and involves five journeys:
From Nazareth to Bethabara. Actual location unknown.
From Bethabara to the Wilderness and return
From Bethabara to Cana and Capernaum
From Capernaum to Jerusalem
From Jerusalem to Sychar and Cana

Insight: *Jesus' first period of ministry covers 15 months, from Jesus' baptism to his rejection at Nazareth, and involves five journeys. Bethany beyond the Jordan is unknown today. It could have been another name for Bethabara or a small town near it. Traditionally, it is placed at a well-known ford east of Jericho.*

Also, there is a well-known ford near Beisan called Abarah, near the mouth of the valley of Jezreel. This is 20 miles from Cana and 60 miles from Bethany. All the conditions of this location fit in with the Biblical history, making it the favored location for Bethabara; it is placed just 13 miles below the Sea of Galilee on the eastern side of the Jordan River.

19 Preaching of John the Baptist

Matthew 3:1-12; Mark 1:2-8; Luke 3:1-17; John 1:19-28

It was the fifteenth year of the rule of Emperor Tiberius; Pontius Pilate was governor of Judea, Herod was ruler of Galilee, and his brother Philip was ruler of the territory of Iturea and Trachonitis; Lysanias was of Abilene, and Annas and Caiaphas were high priests.

At that time the word of God came to John the Baptist son of Zechariah in the desert. John came to the desert of Judea and started preaching and baptizing and went throughout the whole territory of the Jordan River.

"Turn away from your sins and be baptized," he told the people, "and God will forgive your sins, because the Kingdom of heaven is near!"

John's clothes were made of camel's hair; he wore a leather belt around his waist, and his food was locusts and wild honey. People came to him from Jerusalem, from the whole province of Judea, and from all over the country near the Jordan River. They confessed their sins and he baptized them in the Jordan.

People's hopes began to rise, and they began to wonder whether John perhaps might be the Messiah.

The Jewish authorities in Jerusalem sent some priests and Levites to John, to ask him, "Who are you?"

John did not refuse to answer, but spoke out openly and clearly, saying: "I am not the Messiah."

"Who are you then?" they asked. "Are you Elijah?"

"No, I am not," John answered.

"Are you the Prophet?" they asked.

"No," he replied.

"Then tell us who you are," they said. "We have to take an answer back to those who sent us. What do you say about yourself?"

John answered by quoting the prophet Isaiah:

"God said, 'I will send my messenger ahead of you
to open the way for you.'
I am the voice of someone shouting in the desert:
'Get the road ready for the Lord;
make a straight path for him to travel!
Every valley must be filled up,
every hill and mountain leveled off.
The winding roads must be made straight,
and the rough paths made smooth.
The whole human race will see God's salvation!'"
Isaiah 40:3-5; Malachi 3:1 FP

Crowds of people came out to John to be baptized by him. When John saw many Pharisees and Sadducees coming to him to be baptized, he said to them, "You snakes—who told you that you could escape from the punishment God is about to send? Do those things that will show that you have turned from your sins. And don't think you can escape punishment by saying that Abraham is your ancestor.

"I tell you that God can take these rocks and make descendants for Abraham! The ax is ready to cut down the trees at the roots; every tree that does not bear good fruit will be cut down and thrown in the fire. I baptize you with water to show that you have repented, but the one who will come after me will baptize you with the Holy Spirit and fire. He is much greater than I am; and I am not good enough even to carry or untie his sandals. He has his winnowing shovel with him to thresh out all the grain. He will gather his wheat into his barn, but he will burn the chaff in a fire that never goes out."

All this happened in Bethany, on the east side of the Jordan River, where John was baptizing.

The people asked him, "What are we to do, then?"

He answered, "Whoever has two shirts must give one to the man who has none, and whoever has food must share it."

Some tax collectors came to be baptized, and they asked him, " Teacher, what are we to do?"

"Don't collect more than is legal," he told them.

Some soldiers also asked him, "What about us? What are we to do?"

He said to them, "Don't take money from anyone by force or accuse anyone falsely. Be content with your pay."

Insight: *First Journey—When Jesus is about thirty years old, he finally leaves his home town of Nazareth and goes to John in Bethabara to be baptized.*

20 Baptism of Jesus

Matthew 3:13-17; Mark 1:9-11; Luke 3:21-23a

Not long afterward Jesus came from Nazareth in the province of Galilee to John at the Jordan to be baptized by him. But John tried to make him change his mind. "I ought to be baptized by you," John said, "and yet you come to me!"

But Jesus answered him, "Let it be so for now. For in this way we shall do all that God requires." So John agreed. After all the people had been baptized, Jesus also was baptized.

As soon as Jesus was baptized, he came up out of the water. While he was praying, heaven was opened to him, and he saw the Holy Spirit of God coming down upon him in bodily form like a dove and lighting on him. Then a voice said from heaven, "This is my own dear Son, with whom I am pleased."

When Jesus began his work, he was about thirty years old.

Insight: *Second Journey—From Bethabara to the wilderness and return.*

21 Temptation of Jesus

Matthew 4:1-11; Mark 1:12-13; Luke 4:1-13

Jesus returned from the Jordan full of the Holy Spirit and was led by the Spirit into the desert, where he was tempted by the Devil for forty days. In all that time he ate nothing, so that he was hungry when it was over.

Then the Devil came to him and said, "If you are God's Son, order these stones to turn into bread."

But Jesus answered, "The scripture says, 'Human beings cannot live on bread alone, but need every word that God speaks.'"

Then the Devil took Jesus to Jerusalem, the Holy City, set him on the highest point of the Temple, and said to him, "If you are God's Son, throw yourself down from here: For the scripture says,

> 'God will order his angels to take good care of you!' It also says, 'They will hold you up with their hands so that not even your feet will be hurt on the stones.'"

But Jesus answered, "The scripture says, 'Do not put the Lord your God to the test.'"

Then the Devil took Jesus to a very high mountain and showed him in a second all the kingdoms of the world, in all their greatness.

"All this power, and all this wealth I will give you," the Devil said, "if you kneel down and worship me. It has all been handed over to me, and I can give it to anyone I choose."

Then Jesus answered, "Go away, Satan! The scripture says, 'Worship the Lord your God and serve only him!'"

When the Devil finished tempting Jesus in every way, he left him for a while. Wild animals were there also, but angels came and helped him.

22 John's Testimony

John 1:29-34

The next day John saw Jesus coming to him, and said, " There is the Lamb of God, who takes away the sin of the world! This is the one I was talking about when I said, 'A man is coming after me, but he is greater than I am, because he existed before I was born.' I did not know who he would be, but I came baptizing with water in order to make him known to the people of Israel."

And John gave this testimony: "I saw the Spirit come down like a dove from heaven and stay on him.

I still did not know that he was the one, but God, who sent me to baptize with water, had said to me, 'You will see the Spirit come down and stay on a man; he is the one who baptizes with the Holy Spirit.'

I have seen it," said John, "and I tell you that he is the Son of God."

23 First Disciples of Jesus

John 1:35-42

The next day John was standing there again with two of his disciples, when he saw Jesus walking by. "There is the Lamb of God!" he said.

The two disciples heard him say this and went with Jesus. Jesus turned, saw them following him, and asked, "What are you looking for?"

They answered, "Where do you live, Rabbi?" (This word means "Teacher.")

"Come and see," he answered. (It was then about four o'clock in the afternoon.) So they went with him and saw where he lived, and spent the rest of that day with him.

One of them was Andrew, Simon Peter's brother. At once he found his brother Simon and told him, "We have found the Messiah." (This word means "Christ.") Then he took Simon to Jesus. Jesus looked at him and said, "Your name is Simon son of John, but you will be called Cephas." (This is the same as Peter and means "a rock.")

Insight: *Third Journey—From Bethabara to Cana and Capernaum*

24 Philip and Nathanael Called

John 1:43-51

The next day Jesus decided to go to Galilee. He found Philip and said to him, "Come with me!" (Philip was from Bethsaida, the town where Andrew and Peter lived.) Philip found Nathanael and told him, "We have found the one of whom Moses wrote about in the book of the Law and whom the prophets also wrote about. He is Jesus the son of Joseph, from Nazareth."

"Can anything good come from Nazareth?" Nathanael asked.

"Come and see," answered Philip.

When Jesus saw Nathanael coming to him, he said about him, "Here is a real Israelite; there is nothing false in him!"

Nathanael asked him, "How do you know me?"

Jesus answered, "I saw you when you were under the fig tree before Philip called you."

"Teacher," answered Nathanael, "you are the Son of God! You are the King of Israel!"

Jesus said, "Do you believe just because I told you I saw you when you were under the fig tree? You will see much greater things than this!"

And he said to them, "I am telling you the truth: you will see heaven open and God's angels going up and coming down on the Son of Man."

25 Wedding at Cana

John 2:1-12

Two days later there was a wedding in the town of Cana in Galilee. Jesus' mother was there, and Jesus and his disciples had also been invited to the wedding. When the wine had given out, Jesus' mother said to him, "They are out of wine."

"You must not tell me what to do," Jesus replied. "My time has not yet come."

Jesus' mother then told the servants, "Do whatever he tells you."

The Jews have rules about ritual washing, and for this purpose six stone water jars were there, each one large enough to hold between 20 and 30 gallons.

Jesus said to the servants, "Fill these jars with water." They filled them to the brim, and then he told them, "Now draw some water out and take it to the man in charge of the feast."

They took him the water, which now had turned into wine, and he tasted it. He did not know where this wine had come from (but, of course, the servants who had drawn out the water knew); so he called the bridegroom and said to him, "Everyone else serves the best wine first, and after the guests have drunk a lot, he serves the ordinary wine. But you have kept the best wine until now!"

Jesus performed this first miracle in Cana of Galilee; there he revealed his glory, and his disciples believed in him.

After this, Jesus and his mother, brothers, and disciples went to Capernaum and stayed there a few days.

Insight: *Fourth Journey—From Capernaum to Jerusalem to attend the Passover Festival*

26 Jesus Cleanses the Temple

John 2:13-25

It was almost time for the Passover Festival, so Jesus went to Jerusalem. There in the Temple he found men selling cattle, sheep, and pigeons, and also the moneychangers sitting at their tables. So he made a whip from cords and drove all the animals out of the Temple, both the sheep and the cattle; he overturned the tables of the moneychangers and scattered their coins; and he ordered those who sold the pigeons, "Take them out of here! Stop making my Father's house a marketplace!"

His disciples remembered that the scripture says, "My devotion to your house, O God, burns in me like a fire." FP Psalm 69:9

The Jewish authorities came back at him with a question, "What miracle can you perform to show us that you have the right to do this?"

Jesus answered, "Tear down this Temple, and in three days I will build it again."

"Are you going to build it again in three days?" they asked him. "It has taken forty-six years to build this Temple!"

But the temple Jesus was speaking about was his body. So when he was raised from death, his disciples remembered that he said this, and they believed the scripture (FP Psalm 16:10) and what Jesus had said.

While Jesus was in Jerusalem during the Passover Festival, many believed in him as they saw the miracles he performed. But Jesus did not trust himself to them, because he knew them all. There was no need for anyone to tell him about them, because he himself knew what was in their hearts.

27 Jesus and Nicodemus

John 3:1-21

There was a Jewish leader named Nicodemus, who belonged to the party of the Pharisees. One night he went to Jesus and said to him, "Rabbi, we know that you are a teacher sent by God. No one could perform the miracles you are doing unless God were with him."

Jesus answered, "I am telling you the truth: no one can see the Kingdom of God without being born again."

"How can a grown man be born again?" Nicodemus asked. "He certainly cannot enter his mother's womb and be born a second time!"

"I am telling you the truth," replied Jesus, "that no one can enter the Kingdom of God without being born of water and the Spirit. A person is born physically of human parents, but is born spiritually of the Spirit.

Do not be surprised because I tell you that you must all be born again. The wind blows wherever it wishes; you hear the sound it makes, but you do not know where it comes from or where it is going. It is like that with everyone who is born of the Spirit."

"How can this be?" asked Nicodemus.

Jesus answered, "You are a great teacher in Israel, and you don't know this? I am telling you the truth: we speak of what we know and report what we have seen, yet none of you is willing to accept our message. You do not believe me when I tell you about the things of this world; how will you ever believe me, then, when I tell you about the things of heaven? And no one has ever gone up to heaven except the Son of Man, who came down from heaven.

"As Moses lifted up the bronze snake on a pole in the desert, in the same way the Son of Man must be lifted up, so that everyone who believes in him may have eternal life. For God loved the world so much that he gave his only Son, so that everyone who believes in him may not die but have eternal life. For God did not send his Son into the world to be its judge, but to be its savior.

"Those who believe in the Son are not judged; but those who do not believe have already been judged, because they have not believed in God's only Son.

"This is how the judgment works: the light has come into the world, but people love the darkness rather than the light, because their deeds are evil. Those who do evil things hate the light and will not come to the light, because they do not want their evil deeds to be shown up. But those who do what is true come to the light in order that the light may show that what they did was in obedience to God."

Insight: *Fifth Journey - From Jerusalem through Sychar to Cana*

28 Jesus and John

John 3:22-30

After this, Jesus and his disciples went to the province of Judea where he spent some time with them and baptized.

John also was baptizing in Aenon, not far from Salim, because there was plenty of water in that place. People were going to him and he was baptizing them. (This was before John had been put in prison.)

Some of John's disciples began arguing with a Jew about the matter of ritual washing. So they went to John and told him, "Teacher, you remember the man who was with you on the east side of the Jordan, the one you spoke about? Well, he is baptizing now, and everyone is going to him!"

John answered, "No one can have anything unless God gives it. You yourselves are my witnesses that I said, 'I am not the Messiah, but I have been sent ahead of him.'

The bridegroom is the one to whom the bride belongs; but the bridegroom's friend, who stands by and listens, is glad when he hears the bridegroom's voice. This is how my own happiness is made complete. He must become more important while I become less important."

29 He Who Comes from Heaven

John 3:31-36

"He who comes from above is greater than all. He who is from the earth belongs to the earth and speaks about earthly matters, but he who comes from heaven is above all. He tells what he has seen and heard, yet no one accepts his message.

"But whoever accepts his message confirms by this that God is truthful. The one whom God has sent speaks God's words, because God gives him the fullness of his Spirit. The Father loves his Son and has put everything in his power. Whoever believes in the Son has eternal life; whoever disobeys the Son will not have life, but will remain under God's punishment."

30 John and Herod's Wife

Mark 1:14a; Luke 3:18-30

In many different ways John preached the Good News to the people and urged them to change their ways. But John reprimanded Governor Herod, because he had married Herodias, his brother's wife, and had done many other evil things. Then Herod did an even worse thing by putting John in prison.

31 Woman of Samaria

Matthew 4:12; John 4:1-42

The Pharisees heard that Jesus was winning and baptizing more disciples than John. (Actually, Jesus himself did not baptize anyone; only his disciples did.) So when Jesus heard what was being said, and that John had been put in prison, he left Judea and went back to Galilee; on his way there he had to go through Samaria.

In Samaria he came to a town named Sychar, which was not far from the field that Jacob had given to his son Joseph. Jacob's well was there, and Jesus, tired out by the trip, sat down by the well. It was about noon.

A Samaritan woman came to draw some water, and Jesus said to her, "Give me a drink of water." (His disciples had gone into town to buy food.)

The woman answered, "You are a Jew and I am a Samaritan—so how can you ask me for a drink?" (Jews will not use the same cups and bowls that Samaritans use.)

Jesus answered, "If you only knew what God gives and who it is that is asking you for a drink, you would ask him, and he would give you life-giving water."

"Sir," the woman said, "you don't have a bucket and the well is deep. Where would you get that life-giving water?

It was our ancestor Jacob who gave us this well; he and his children and his flocks all drank from it. You don't claim to be greater than Jacob, do you?"

Jesus answered, "Those who drink this water will get thirsty again; but those who drink the water that I will give them will never be thirsty again. The water that I will give them will become in them a spring which will provide them with life-giving water and give them eternal life."

"Sir," the woman said, "give me that water! Then I will never be thirsty again, nor will I have to come here to draw water."

"Go and call your husband," Jesus told her, "and come back."

"I don't have a husband," she answered.

Jesus replied, "You are right when you say you don't have a husband. You have been married to five men, and the man you live with now is not really your husband. You have told me the truth."

"I see you are a prophet, sir," the woman said. "My Samaritan ancestors worshiped God on this mountain, but you Jews say that Jerusalem is the place where we should worship God."

Jesus said to her, "Believe me, woman, the time will come when people will not worship the Father either on this mountain or in Jerusalem. You Samaritans do not really know whom you worship; but we Jews know whom we worship, because it is from the Jews that salvation comes.

"But the time is coming and is already here, when by the power of God's Spirit people will worship the Father as he really is, offering him the true worship that he wants.

"God is Spirit, and only by the power of his Spirit can people worship him as he really is."

The woman said to him, "I know that the Messiah will come, and when he comes, he will tell us everything."

Jesus answered, "I am he, I who am talking with you."

At that moment Jesus' disciples returned, and they were greatly surprised to find him talking with a woman.

But none of them said to her, "What do you want?" or asked him, "Why are you talking with her?"

Then the woman left her water jar, went back to the town, and said to the people there, "Come and see the man who told me everything I have ever done. Could he be the Messiah?" So they left the town and went to Jesus.

In the meantime the disciples were begging Jesus, "Teacher, have something to eat!"

But he answered, "I have food to eat that you know nothing about."

So the disciples started asking among themselves, "Could somebody have brought him food?"

"My food," Jesus said to them, "is to obey the will of the one who sent me and to finish the work he gave me to do.

"You have a saying, 'Four more months and then the harvest.' But I tell you, take a good look at the fields; the crops are now ripe and ready to be harvested!

The one who reaps the harvest is being paid and gathers the crops for eternal life; so the one who plants and the one who reaps will be glad together.

"For the saying is true, 'Someone plants, someone else reaps.' I have sent you to reap a harvest in a field where you did not work; others worked there, and you profit from their work."

Many of the Samaritans in that town believed in Jesus because the woman had said, "He told me everything I have ever done." So when the Samaritans came to him, they begged him to stay with them, and Jesus stayed there two days.

Many more believed because of his message, and they told the woman, "We believe now, not because of what you said, but because we ourselves have heard him, and we know that he is really the Savior of the world."

III. EARLY GALILEAN MINISTRY

The period from Jesus' birth to his baptism covers thirty years and involves four journeys:

From Bethlehem to Jerusalem and return

From Bethlehem to Egypt where He remained until Herod's death

From Egypt to Nazareth

From Nazareth to Jerusalem for the Passover Festival and return when he was 12 years old.

There is no Biblical record of Jesus' life from this time until his baptism when he was about 30 years old.

Insight: The Early Galilean Ministry, a period of about four months, covers the period from his arrival in Cana and his rejection at Nazareth to the Sermon on the Mount and involves four journeys.

32 Jesus Begins in Galilee

Luke 4:14-15; John 4:43-45

After spending two days there [*Samaria*], Jesus left and went to Galilee. For he himself had said, "Prophets are not respected in their own country."

When he arrived in Galilee, the people there welcomed him, because they had gone to the Passover Festival in Jerusalem and had seen everything that he had done during the festival.

The news about him spread throughout all that territory. He taught in the synagogues and was praised by everyone.

Insight: *First journey - Cana to Nazareth, then moved to Capernaum.*

33 Jesus Heals Official's Son

John 4:46-54

Then Jesus went back to Cana in Galilee, where he had turned the water into wine. A government official was there whose son was sick in Capernaum. When he heard that Jesus had come from Judea to Galilee, he went to him and asked him to go to Capernaum and heal his son, who was about to die. Jesus said to him, "None of you will ever believe unless you see miracles and wonders."

"Sir," replied the official, "come with me before my child dies."

Jesus said to him, "Go; your son will live!"

The man believed Jesus' words and went. On his way home his servants met him with the news, "Your boy is going to live!"

He asked them what time it was when his son got better, and they answered, "It was one o'clock yesterday afternoon when the fever left him."

Then the father remembered that it was at that very hour when Jesus had told him, "Your son will live." So he and all his family believed.

This was the second miracle that Jesus performed after coming from Judea to Galilee.

Insight: *This was the second miracle that Jesus performed in Galilee but was not the second miracle of his ministry! On Jesus' previous trip to Jerusalem, when he cleansed the Temple, Jesus performed many miracles there.* *John 2:23-25*

34 Rejection at Nazareth

Matthew 13:54-58; Mark 6:1-6a; Luke 4:16-30

Then Jesus went to Nazareth, where he had been brought up, and on the Sabbath he went as usual to the synagogue. He stood up to read the Scriptures and was handed the book of the prophet Isaiah. He unrolled the scroll and found the place where it is written,

"The Spirit of the Lord is upon me,
because he has chosen me to bring
good news to the poor.

He has sent me to proclaim liberty to the
captives and recovery of sight to the blind,
to set free the oppressed and announce
that the time has come when the Lord
will save his people."

Jesus rolled up the scroll, gave it back to the attendant, and sat down. All the people in the synagogue had their eyes fixed on him, as he said to them, "This passage of scripture has come true today, as you heard it being read."

They were all well impressed with him, and marveled at the eloquent words that he spoke. They said, "Where did he get all this?" they asked. "What wisdom is this that has been given him? How does he perform miracles? Isn't he the carpenter, son of Joseph and Mary, and the brother of James, Joseph, Judas, and Simon?

"Aren't his sisters living here?" And so they rejected him.

Jesus said to them, "Prophets are respected everywhere except in their own hometown and by their relatives and their family."

He was not able to perform any miracles there, except that he placed his hands on a few sick people and healed them. He was greatly surprised, because the people did not have faith.

He said to them, "I am sure that you will quote this proverb to me, 'Doctor, heal yourself.'

"You will also tell me to do here in my hometown the same things you heard were done in Capernaum.

"Listen to me: it is true that there were many widows in Israel during the time of Elijah, when there was no rain for three and half years and a severe famine spread throughout the whole land. Yet Elijah was not sent to anyone in Israel, but only to a widow living in Zarephath in the territory of Sidon.

"And there were many people suffering from a dreaded skin disease who lived in Israel during the time of the prophet Elisha; yet not one of them was healed, but only Naaman the Syrian."

When the people in the synagogue heard this, they were filled with anger. They rose up, dragged Jesus out of town, and took him to the top of the hill on which their town was built. They meant to throw him over the cliff, but he walked through the middle of the crowd and went his way.

35 Jesus Moves to Capernaum

Matthew 4:13-17; Mark 11:4b-15

He did not stay in Nazareth, but went to live in Capernaum, a town by Lake Galilee, in the territory of Zebulun and Naphtali. This was done to make come true what the prophet Isaiah had said,

"Land of Zebulun, and land of Naphtali,
on the road to the sea,
on the other side of the Jordan,
Galilee, land of the Gentiles!
The people who live in darkness
will see a great light.
On those who live in the dark land of death
the light will shine." FP Is. 9:1-2

From that time Jesus began to preach his message, "The right time has come," he said," and the Kingdom of God is near! Turn away from your sins and believe the Good News!"

36 Jesus Calls Four Fishermen

Matthew 3:18-22; Mark 1:16-20; Luke 5:1-11

One day Jesus was standing on the shore of Lake Galilee while the people pushed their way up to him to listen to the word of God. He saw two boats pulled up on the beach; the fishermen had left them and were washing the nets.

Jesus got into one of the boats, it belonged to Simon, and asked him to push off a little from the shore. Jesus sat in the boat and taught the crowd.

When he finished speaking, he said to Simon, "Push the boat out further to the deep water, and you and your partners let your nets down for a catch."

"Master," Simon answered, "we worked hard all night long and caught nothing. But if you say so, I will let down the nets."

They let them down and caught such a large number of fish that the nets were about to break.

So they motioned to their partners in the other boat to come and help them. They came and filled both boats so full of fish that the boats were about to sink.

When Simon Peter saw what had happened, he fell on his knees before Jesus and said, "Go away from me, Lord! I am a sinful man!"

He and the others with him were all amazed at the large number of fish they had caught. The same was true of Simon's partners, James and John, the sons of Zebedee.

Jesus said to Simon (called Peter) and his brother Andrew, "Don't be afraid; come with me and from now on I will teach you to catch people."

At once they left their nets. They pulled the boats up on the beach, left everything, and followed Jesus.

He went a little farther on and saw two other brothers, James and John, the sons of Zebedee. They were in their boat with their father Zebedee, getting their nets ready. As soon as Jesus saw them, he called them. They left their father Zebedee in the boat with the hired men and went with Jesus.

37 Man with an Evil Spirit

Matthew 1:21-28; Luke 4:31-37

Then Jesus and his disciples went to Capernaum, a town in Galilee, where he went to the synagogue and taught the people on the Sabbath. The people who heard him were all amazed at the way he taught, for he wasn't like the teachers of the Law; instead, he taught with authority.

Just then a man with an evil spirit came into the synagogue and screamed out in a loud voice, "Ah! What do you want with us, Jesus of Nazareth? Are you here to destroy us? I know who you are: you are God's holy messenger!"

Jesus ordered the spirit, "Be quiet and come out of the man!"

The evil spirit shook the man hard, threw the man down in front of them, gave a loud scream and went out of him without doing him any harm.

The people were all so amazed that they started saying to one another, "What is this? What kind of words are these? Is it some kind of new teaching?

"With authority and power this man gives orders to the evil spirits, and they obey him and they come out!"

And so the news about Jesus spread quickly everywhere in the province of Galilee.

38 Peter's Mother-in-Law

Matthew 8:14-17; Mark 1:29-34; Luke 4:38-41

Jesus and his disciples, including James and John, left the synagogue and went straight to the home of Simon and Andrew. Simon's mother-in-law was sick in bed with a high fever, and as soon as Jesus arrived, he was told about her. He went and stood at her bedside, took her by the hand, ordered the fever to leave her and helped her up. The fever left her, and she got up at once and began to wait on them.

After the sun had set and evening had come, all who had friends who were sick with various diseases brought them to Jesus. All the people of the town gathered in front of the house. He placed his hands on every one of them and healed them all. He did this to make come true what the prophet Isaiah had said,

"He himself took our sickness and carried
away our diseases." FP Isaiah 53:4

Jesus drove out the evil spirits with a word and they went out from many people screaming, "You are the Son of God!"

Jesus gave the demons an order and would not let them speak, because they knew he was the Messiah.

Insight: Second Journey - From Capernaum through Eastern Galilee and return. At that time the land of Galilee was all around Lake Galilee. Travelers often crossed the lake by boat rather than walk around the top end of the lake.

39 Jesus in Eastern Galilee

Matthew 4:23-25; Mark 1:35-39; Luke 4:42-44

Very early the next morning, long before daylight, Jesus got up and left the house. He went out of town to a lonely place, where he prayed. But Simon and his companions went out searching for him, and when they found him, they said, "Everyone is looking for you." And they tried to keep him from leaving.

But he said to them, "I must preach the Good News about the Kingdom of God in other towns also, because that is what God sent me to do."

So he traveled all over Galilee, teaching in the synagogues, preaching the Good News about the Kingdom, and healing people who had all kinds of disease and sickness.

The news about him spread through the whole country of Syria, so that people brought to him all those who were sick, suffering from all kinds of diseases and disorders: people with demons, and epileptics, and paralytics, and Jesus healed them all. Large crowds followed him from Galilee and the Ten Towns, from Jerusalem, Judea, and the land on the other side of the Jordan.

40 A Leper Made Clean

Matthew 8:2-4; Mark 1:40-45; Luke 5:12-16

Once Jesus was in a town where there was a man who was suffering from a dreaded skin disease.

When he saw Jesus, he threw himself down and begged him, "Sir, if you want to, you can make me clean!"

Jesus was filled with pity, and reached out and touched him. "I do want to," he answered. "Be clean!" At once the disease left the man, and he was clean.

Then Jesus spoke sternly to him and sent him away at once, after saying to him, "Listen, don't tell anyone about this. But go straight to the priest and let him examine you; then in order to prove to everyone that you are cured, offer the sacrifice that Moses ordered."

But the man went away and began to spread the news everywhere. Indeed, he talked so much that Jesus could not go into a town publicly. Instead he would go away to lonely places, where he prayed, and people came to him from everywhere to hear him and be healed from their diseases.

41 Paralyzed Man Healed

Matthew 9:1-8; Mark 2:1-12; Luke 5:17-26;

A few days later Jesus went back to Capernaum, and the news spread that he was at home. So many people came together that there was no room left, not even out in front of the door.

Jesus was preaching the message to them. Some Pharisees and teachers of the Law were sitting there who had come from every town in Galilee and Judea and from Jerusalem. The power of the Lord was present for Jesus to heal the sick.

Four men came carrying a paralyzed man on a bed, and they tried to carry him into the house and put him in front of Jesus. Because of the crowd, however, they could find no way to take him in.

So they carried him up on the roof, right above the place where Jesus was, made an opening in the tiles, and let him down on his bed into the middle of the group in front of Jesus.

When Jesus saw how much faith they had, he said to the paralyzed man, "Courage, my son! (my friend). Your sins are forgiven."

The teachers of the Law and the Pharisees began to say to themselves, "Who is this man who speaks such blasphemy! How does he dare talk like this?

"God is the only one who can forgive sins!"

At once Jesus knew what they were thinking, so he said to them, "Why do you think such evil things?

"Is it easier to say to this paralyzed man, 'Your sins are forgiven,' or to say, 'Get up, pick up your mat, and walk. I will prove to you, then, that the Son of Man has authority on earth to forgive sins." So he said to the paralyzed man, "Get up, pick up your mat, and walk."

While they all watched, the man got up in front of them all, took the bed he had been lying on, and hurried home, praising God. They were all completely amazed!

Full of fear, they praised God for giving such authority to people saying, "What marvelous things we have seen today! We have never seen anything like this!"

42 Jesus Calls Matthew

Matthew 9:9-13; Mark 2:13-17; Luke 5:27-32

After this, Jesus left that place and went back again to the shore of Lake Galilee. A crowd came to him, and he started teaching them. As he walked along, he saw a tax collector, Levi son of Alphaeus, sitting in his office. Jesus said to him, "Follow me." Levi got up, left everything and followed him.

Later on Levi had a big feast in his house for Jesus. Many tax collectors and other outcasts came and joined Jesus and his disciples at the table.

Some Pharisees and some teachers of the Law who belonged to their group saw that Jesus was eating with these outcasts and tax collectors, so they complained to Jesus' disciples. "Why does your teacher eat and drink with tax collectors and other outcasts?" they asked.

Jesus heard them and answered, "People who are well do not need a doctor, but only those who are sick. Go and find out what is meant by the scripture that says: 'It is kindness that I want, not animal sacrifices.' I have not come to call respectable people to repent, but outcasts."

Insight: *Third Journey - From Capernaum to Jerusalem for a religious festival and return.*

43 The Healing at the Pool

John 5:1-18

After this, Jesus went to Jerusalem for a religious festival. Near the Sheep Gate in Jerusalem there is a pool with five porches; in Hebrew it is called Bethzatha.

A large crowd of sick people were lying on the porches; the blind, the lame, and the paralyzed.

INSIGHT: *Some manuscripts say: "They were waiting for the water to move, because every now and then an angel of the Lord went down into the pool and stirred up the water. The first sick person to go into the pool after the water was stirred up was healed from whatever disease he had."*

A man was there who had been sick for thirty-eight years. Jesus saw him lying there, and he knew that the man had been sick for such a long time; so he asked him, "Do you want to get well?"

The sick man answered, "Sir, I don't have anyone here to put me in the pool when the water is stirred up; while I am trying to get in, somebody else gets there first. "Jesus said to him, "Get up, pick up your mat, and walk."

Immediately the man got well; he picked up his mat and started walking.

The day this happened was a Sabbath, so the Jewish authorities told the man who had been healed, "This is a Sabbath, and it is against our Law for you to carry your mat."

He answered, "The man who made me well told me to pick up my mat and walk."

They asked him, "Who is the man who told you to do this?"

But the man who had been healed did not know who Jesus was, for there was a crowd in that place, and Jesus had slipped away.

Afterward, Jesus found him in the Temple and said, "Listen, you are well now; so stop sinning or something worse may happen to you."

Then the man left and told the Jewish authorities that it was Jesus who had healed him. So they began to persecute Jesus, because he had done this healing on a Sabbath. Jesus answered them, "My Father is always working, and I too must work."

This saying made the Jewish authorities all the more determined to kill him; not only had he broken the Sabbath law, but he had said that God was his own Father and in this way had made himself equal with God.

44 The Authority of the Son

John 5:19-47

So Jesus answered them, "I tell you the truth: the Son can do nothing on his own; he does only what he sees his Father doing. What the Father does, the Son also does. For the Father loves the Son and shows him all that he himself is doing. He will show him even greater things to do than this, and you will all be amazed.

"Just as the Father raises the dead and gives them life, in the same way the Son gives life to those he wants to. Nor does the Father himself judge anyone. He has given his Son the full right to judge, so that all will honor the Son in the same way as they honor the Father.

"Whoever does not honor the Son does not honor the Father who sent him.

"I am telling you the truth: those who hear my words and believe in him who sent me have eternal life. They will not be judged, but have already passed from death to life.

"I am telling you the truth: the time is coming - the time has already come - when the dead will hear the voice of the Son of God, and those who hear it will come to life.

"Just as the Father is himself the source of life, in the same way he has made his Son to be source of life. And he has given the Son the right to judge, because he is the Son of Man.

"Do not be surprised at this; the time is coming when all the dead will hear his voice and come out of their graves: those who have done good will rise and live, and those who have done evil will rise and be condemned.

"I can do nothing on my own authority; I judge only as God tells me, so my judgment is right, because I am not trying to do what I want, but only what he who sent me wants.

"If I testify on my own behalf, what I say is not to be accepted as real proof. But there is someone else who testifies on my behalf, and I know that what he says about me is true. John is the one to whom you sent your messengers, and he spoke on behalf of the truth. It is not that I must have a human witness; I say this only in order that you may be saved. John was like a lamp, burning and shining, and you were willing for a while to enjoy his light.

"But I have a witness on my behalf which is even greater than the witness that John gave: what I do, that is, the deeds that my Father gave me to do, these speak on my behalf and show that the Father has sent me. And the Father, who sent me, also testifies on my behalf. You have never heard his voice or seen his face, and you do not keep his message in your hearts, for you do not believe in the one whom he sent. You study the Scriptures, because you think that in them you will find eternal life. And these very Scriptures speak about me! Yet you are not willing to come to me in order to have life.

"I am not looking for human praise. But I know what kind of people you are, and I know that you have no love for God in your hearts. I have come with my Father's authority, but you have not received me; when, however, someone comes with his own authority, you will receive him.

"You like to receive praise from one another, but you do not try to win praise from the one who alone is God; how, then, can you believe me?

"Do not think, however, that I am the one who will accuse you to my Father.

"Moses, in whom you have put your hope, is the very one who will accuse you. If you had really believed Moses, you would have believed me, because he wrote about me. But since you do not believe what he wrote, how can you believe what I say?"

45 Question about Fasting

Matthew 9:14-15; Mark 2:18-20; Luke 5:33-35

On one occasion the followers of John the Baptist and the Pharisees were fasting. Then the followers of John the Baptist came to Jesus asking, "Why is it that the disciples of John the Baptist and the disciples of the Pharisees fast frequently and offer up prayers, but your disciples don't fast at all; your disciples eat and drink."

Jesus answered, "Do you expect the guests at a wedding party to be sad and go without food as long as the bridegroom is with them? Of course not!

"As long as the bridegroom is with them they will not do that.

"But the day will come when the bridegroom will be taken away from them, and then they will fast."

46 New Patch on Old Fabric

Matthew 9:16-17; Mark 2:21-22; Luke 5:36-39

Jesus also told them this parable: "You don't tear a piece off a new coat to patch up an old coat. If you do, you will have torn the new coat, and the piece of new cloth will not match the old because the new patch will shrink and tear off some of the old cloth, making an even bigger hole.

"Nor does anyone pour new wine into used wineskins, because the wine will burst the skins, and both the wine and the skins will be ruined. Instead, new wine is poured into fresh wineskins, and both will keep in good condition. And you don't want new wine after drinking old wine. 'The old is better,' you say."

47 Question about the Sabbath

Matthew 12:1-8; Mark 2:23-28; Luke 6:1-5

Not long afterward Jesus was walking through some wheat fields on a Sabbath. His disciples were hungry. As his disciples walked along with him, they began to pick the heads of wheat, rub them in their hands, and eat the grain. When the Pharisees saw this, they said to Jesus, "Look, it is against our Law for your disciples to do this on the Sabbath!"

Jesus answered them, "Haven't you read what David did when he and his men were hungry? He went into the house of God, and he and his men ate the bread offered to God, even though it was against the Law for them to eat it? Only the priests were allowed to eat that bread.

"This happened when Abiathar was the High Priest.

"Or have you not read in the Law of Moses that every Sabbath the priests in the Temple actually break the Sabbath law, yet they are not guilty?

"I tell you that there is something here greater than the Temple. The scripture says, 'It is kindness that I want, not animal sacrifices.'

"If you really knew what this means, you would not condemn people who are not guilty."

And Jesus concluded, "The Sabbath was made for the good of human beings; they were not made for the Sabbath. So the Son of Man is Lord even of the Sabbath."

48 Man with a Paralyzed Hand

Matthew 12:9-14; Mark 3:1-6; Luke 6:6-11

On another Sabbath Jesus went into a synagogue and taught. A man was there whose right hand was paralyzed.

Some teachers of the Law and some Pharisees wanted a reason to accuse Jesus of doing wrong, so they watched him closely to see if he would heal on the Sabbath.

They asked him, "Is it against our Law to heal on the Sabbath?"

But Jesus knew their thoughts and said to the man, "Stand up and come here to the front." The man got up and stood there. Then Jesus said to them, "I ask you: What does our Law allow us to do on the Sabbath? To help or to harm? To save a man's life or destroy it? What if one of you has a sheep and it falls into a deep hole on the Sabbath? Will he not take hold of it and lift it out? And a man is worth much more than a sheep! So then, our Law does allow us to help someone on the Sabbath."

He looked around at them all, but they did not say a thing. Jesus was angry as he looked around at them, but at the same time he felt sorry for them, because they were so stubborn and wrong. Then he said to the man, "Stretch out your hand." He stretched it out and it became well again, just like the other one.

Then the Pharisees left the synagogue. They were filled with rage and began to discuss among themselves what they could do to Jesus. The Pharisees met at once with some members of Herod's party, and they made plans to kill Jesus.

49 God's Chosen Servant

Matthew 12:15-21

When Jesus heard about the plot against him, he went away from that place; and large crowds followed him.

He healed all the sick, and gave them orders not to tell others about him.

He did this so as to make come true what God had said through the prophet Isaiah:

"Here is my servant, whom I have chosen,
the one I love, and with whom I am pleased.
I will send my Spirit upon him,
and he will announce my judgment to the nations.

He will not argue or shout,
or make loud speeches in the streets.

He will not break off a bent reed,
nor put out a flickering lamp.

He will persist until he causes justice to triumph,
and on him all the peoples will put their hope." FP Isaiah 42:1

Insight: *Fourth Journey - From Capernaum to the mountain where he preaches The Sermon on the Mount and return.*

50 A Crowd by the Lake

Mark 3:7-12

Jesus and his disciples went away to Lake Galilee, and a large crowd followed him.

They had come from Galilee, from Judea, from Jerusalem, from the territory of Idumea, from the territory on the east side of the Jordan, and from the region around the cities of Tyre and Sidon. All these people came to Jesus because they heard of the things he was doing.

The crowd was so large that Jesus told his disciples to get a boat ready for him, so that the people would not crush him. He had healed many people, and all the sick kept pushing their way to him in order to touch him. And whenever the people who had evil spirits in them saw him, they would fall down before him and scream, "You are the Son of God!"

Jesus sternly ordered the evil spirits not to tell anyone who he was.

51 Twelve Apostles Chosen

Matthew 10:1-4; Mark 3:13-19; Luke 6:12-16

Then Jesus went up a hill to pray and spent the whole night there praying to God. When day came, he called his disciples to him and chose twelve of them, whom he named apostles. "I have chosen you to be with me," he told them. "I will also send you out to preach, and you will have authority to drive out demons and to heal every disease and every sickness."

These are the names of the twelve apostles: first, Simon (called Peter) and his brother Andrew; James and his brother John, the sons of Zebedee (Jesus gave them the name Boanerges, which means "Men of Thunder"; Philip and Bartholomew; Thomas and Matthew, the tax collector; James son of Alphaeus, and Thaddaeus; Simon the Patriot and Judas Iscariot, who became the traitor who betrayed Jesus.

52 Jesus Teaches and Heals

Matthew 5:1-2; Luke 6:17-19

When Jesus had come down from the hill with the apostles, he stood on a level place with a large number of his disciples. A large crowd of people was there from all over Judea and from Jerusalem and from the coast cities of Tyre and Sidon; they had come to hear him and to be healed of their diseases. Those who were troubled by evil spirits also came and were healed. All the people tried to touch him, for power was going out from him and healing them all.

Jesus saw the crowds and went up a hill, where he sat down. His disciples gathered around him, and he began to teach them.

53 True Happiness

Matthew 5:3-12; Luke 6:20-26

Jesus looked at his disciples and said:

"Happy are those who know they are spiritually poor; the Kingdom of heaven belongs to them!

"Happy are those who mourn, who weep now; God will comfort them!

"They will laugh!

"Happy are those who are humble; they will receive what God has promised!

"Happy are those whose greatest desire is to do what God requires; God will satisfy them fully!

"Happy are those who are hungry now; they will be filled!

"Happy are those who are merciful to others; God will be merciful to them!

"Happy are the pure in heart; they will see God!

"Happy are those who work for peace; God will call them his children!

"Happy are those who are persecuted because they do what God requires; the Kingdom of heaven belongs to them!

"Happy are you when people insult you and persecute you, hate you, reject you, and say that you are evil and tell all kinds of evil lies against you because you are my followers.

"Be happy and glad when that happens and dance for joy, because a great reward is kept for you in heaven.

"This is how the prophets who lived before you were persecuted.

"But how terrible for you who are rich now; you have had your easy life!

"How terrible for you who are full now; you will go hungry!

"How terrible for you who laugh now; you will mourn and weep!

"How terrible when all people speak well of you; their ancestors said the very same things about the false prophets."

54 Salt

Matthew 5:13; Mark 9:49-50; Luke 14:34-35

"Everyone will be purified by fire as a sacrifice is purified by salt. You are like salt for the whole human race.

"Salt is good, but if it loses its saltiness, there is no way to make it salty again. It has become worthless. It is no good for the soil or for the manure pile; it is thrown away and people trample on it. Listen, then, if you have ears!

"Have the salt of friendship among yourselves, and live in peace with one another."

55 Law

Matthew 5:17-20

"Do not think that I have come to do away with the Law of Moses and the teachings of the prophets.

"I have not come to do away with them, but to make their teachings come true. Remember that as long as heaven and earth last, not the least point nor the smallest detail of the Law will be done away with - not until the end of all things.

"So then, whoever disobeys even the least important of the commandments and teaches others to do the same, will be least in the Kingdom of heaven.

"On the other hand, whoever obeys the law and teaches others to do the same, will be great in the Kingdom of heaven. I tell you, then, that you will be able to enter the Kingdom of heaven only if you are more faithful than the teachers of the Law and the Pharisees in doing what God requires."

56 Anger

Matthew 5:21-26; Luke 12:57-59

"You have heard that people were told in the past, 'Do not commit murder; anyone who does will be brought to trial.' But now I tell you: if you are angry with your brother you will be brought to trial; if you call your brother 'You good-for-nothing!' you will be brought before the Council, and if you call your brother a worthless fool you will be in danger of going to the fire of hell.

"So if you are about to offer your gift to God at the altar and there you remember that your brother has something against you, leave your gift there in front of the altar, go at once and make peace with your brother, and then come back and offer your gift to God.

"Why do you not judge for yourselves the right thing to do? If someone brings a lawsuit against you and takes you to court, do your best to settle the dispute while there is time, before you get to court. If you don't, you will be dragged before the judge, who will hand you over to the police, and you will be put in jail.

"There you will stay, I tell you, until you pay the last penny of your fine."

57 Adultery

Matthew 5:27-30

"You have heard that it was said, 'Do not commit adultery.' But now I tell you: anyone who looks at a woman and wants to possess her is guilty of committing adultery with her in his heart. So if your right eye causes you to sin, take it out and throw it away!

"It is much better for you to lose a part of your body than to have your whole body thrown into hell.

"If your right hand causes you to sin, cut it off and throw it away! It is much better for you to lose one of your limbs than to have your whole body go off to hell."

58 Divorce

Matthew 5:31-32; Luke 16:18

"It was also said, 'Anyone who divorces his wife must give her a written notice of divorce.'

"But now I tell you: if a man divorces his wife for any cause other than her unfaithfulness, then he is guilty of making her commit adultery if she marries again; and the man who marries her commits adultery also."

59 Vows

Matthew 5:33-37

"You have also heard that men were told in the past, 'Do not break your promise, but do what you have vowed to the Lord to do.' But now I tell you: do not use any vow when you make a promise.

"Do not swear by heaven, for it is God's throne; nor by earth, for it is the resting place for his feet; nor by Jerusalem, for it is the city of the great King. Do not even swear by your head, because you cannot make a single hair white or black. Just say 'Yes' or 'No.' Anything else you say comes from the Evil One."

60 Love for Enemies

Matthew 5:38-48; Luke 6:27-36

"You have heard that it was said, 'An eye for an eye, and a tooth for a tooth.' But now I tell you: do not take revenge on someone who wrongs you.

"If anyone slaps you on the right cheek, let him slap your left cheek too. And if someone takes you to court to sue you for your shirt, let him have your coat as well.

"And if one of the occupation troops forces you to carry his pack one mile, carry it two miles. When someone asks you for something, give it to him; when someone wants to borrow something, lend it to him." Give to everyone who asks you for something, and when someone takes what is yours, do not ask for it back. Do for others just what you want them to do for you.

"You have heard that it was said, 'Love your friends, hate your enemies.' But I tell you who hear me: Love your enemies, do good to those who hate you, bless those who curse you, and pray for those who mistreat and persecute you, so that you may become the children of your Father in heaven. For he makes his sun to shine on bad and good people alike, and gives rain to those who do good and to those who do evil. Why should God reward you if you love only the people who love you? Even sinners and tax collectors do that! And if you speak only to your friends, have you done anything out of the ordinary? Even the pagans do that!

"And if you do good only to those who do good to you, why should you receive a blessing? Even sinners do that! And if you lend only to those from whom you hope to get it back, why should you receive a blessing? Even sinners lend to sinners, to get back the same amount!

"No! Love your enemies and do good to them; lend and expect nothing back. You will then have a great reward, and you will be children of the Most High God. For he is good to the ungrateful and the wicked.

"Be merciful, just as your Father is merciful. You must be perfect just as your Father in heaven is perfect!"

61 Charity

Matthew 6:1-4

"Make certain you do not perform your religious duties in public so that people will see what you do. If you do these things publicly, you will not have any reward from your Father in heaven.

"So when you give something to a needy person, do not make a big show of it, as the hypocrites do in the houses of worship and on the streets. They do it so that people will praise them. I assure you, they have already been paid in full.

"But when you help a needy person, do it in such a way that even your closest friend will not know about it. Then it will be a private matter. And your Father, who sees what you do in private, will reward you."

62 Prayer

Matthew 6:5-15; Luke 11:1-8

One day Jesus was praying in a certain place. When he had finished, one of his disciples said to him, "Lord, teach us to pray, just as John taught his disciples."

Jesus said to them, "When you pray, do not be like the hypocrites! They love to stand up and pray in the houses of worship and on the street corners, so that everyone will see them. I assure you, they have already been paid in full.

"But when you pray, go to your room, close the door, and pray to your Father, who is unseen. And your Father, who sees what you do in private, will reward you.

"When you pray, do not use a lot of meaningless words, as the pagans do, who think that their gods will hear them because their prayers are long. Do not be like them. Your Father already knows what you need before you ask him.

This, then, is how you should pray:

"'Our Father in heaven: May your holy name be honored,
may your Kingdom come;
may your will be done on earth as it is in heaven.
Give us day by day the food we need.

Forgive us our sins and the wrongs we have done,
as we forgive the wrong that others have done to us.
Do not bring us to hard testing,
but keep us safe from the Evil One!'"

"If you forgive others the wrongs they have done to you, your Father in heaven will also forgive you. But if you do not forgive others, then your Father will not forgive the wrongs you have done."

And Jesus said to his disciples, "Suppose one of you should go to a friend's house at midnight and say, 'Friend, let me borrow three loaves of bread. A friend of mine who is on a trip has just come to my house, and I don't have any food for him!' And suppose your friend should answer from inside, 'Don't bother me! The door is already locked, and my children and I are in bed. I can't get up and give you anything.'

"Well, what then? I tell you that even if he will not get up and give you the bread because you are his friend, yet he will get up and give you everything you need because you are not ashamed to keep on asking."

63 Teaching about Fasting

Matthew 6:16-18

"And when you fast, do not put on a sad face as the hypocrites do. They neglect their appearance so that everyone will see that they are fasting.

"I assure you, they have already been paid in full.

"When you go without food, wash your face and comb your hair, so that others cannot know that you are fasting - only your Father, who is unseen, will know. And your Father, who sees what you do in private, will reward you."

64 Riches in Heaven

Matthew 6:19-21; Luke 12:32-34

"Do not be afraid, little flock, for your Father is pleased to give you the Kingdom. Sell all your belongings and give the money to the poor. Provide for yourselves purses that don't wear out.

"Do not store up riches for yourselves here on earth, where moths and rust destroy, and robbers break in and steal. Instead, store up riches for yourselves in heaven, where they will never decrease, where moths and rust cannot destroy, and robbers cannot break in and steal.

"For your heart will always be where your riches are."

65 The Light of the Body

Matthew 5:14-16; 6:22-23; Luke 11:33-36

"You are like light for the whole world.

"A city built on a hill cannot be hid. No one lights a lamp and then hides it or puts it under a bowl; instead it is put on the lamp stand, where it gives light for everyone in the house. In the same way your light must shine before people, so that they will see the good things you do and praise your Father in heaven.

"Your eyes are like a lamp for the body. When your eyes are sound, your whole body is full of light; but when your eyes are no good, your whole body will be in darkness.

"Make certain, then, that the light in you is not darkness.

"If the light in you is darkness, how terribly dark it will be! If your whole body is full of light, with no part of it in darkness, it will be bright all over, as when a lamp shines on you with its brightness."

66 God and Possessions

Matthew 6:24-34; Luke 12:22-31; 16:13

"No servant can be the slave of two masters; such a slave will hate one and love the other or will be loyal to one and despise the other. You cannot serve both God and money.

"This is why I tell you: do not be worried about the food and drink you need in order to stay alive, or about clothes for your body.

"After all, isn't life worth more than food? And isn't the body worth more than clothes? Look at the birds: they do not plant seeds, gather a harvest and put it in barns; yet your Father in heaven takes care of them! Aren't you worth much more than birds? Can any of you live a bit longer by worrying about it? If you can't manage even such a small thing, why worry about the other things?

"And why worry about clothes? Look how the wild flowers grow: they do not work or make clothes for themselves. But I tell you that not even King Solomon with all his wealth had clothes as beautiful as one of these flowers. It is God who clothes the wild grass - grass that is here today and gone tomorrow, burned up in the oven. Won't he be all the more sure to clothe you? What little faith you have!

"So do not start worrying: 'Where will my food come from? or my drink? or my clothes?' (These are the things the pagans are always concerned about.) Your Father in heaven knows that you need all these things. Instead, be concerned above everything else with the Kingdom of God and with what he requires of you, and he will provide you with all these other things. So do not worry about tomorrow; it will have enough worries of its own. There is no need to add to the troubles each day brings."

67 Judging Others

Matthew 7:1-6; Luke 6:37-42

"Do not judge others, so that God will not judge you, for God will judge you in the same way you judge others, and he will apply to you the same rules you apply to others. Do not condemn others, and God will not condemn you; forgive others, and God will forgive you.

"Give to others, and God will give to you. Indeed, you will receive a full measure, a generous helping, poured into your hands - all that you can hold. The measure that you use for others is the one God will use for you."

And Jesus told them this parable, "One blind man cannot lead another one; if he does, both will fall into a ditch. No pupils are greater than their teacher; but all pupils, when they have completed their training, will be like their teacher.

"Why do you look at the speck in your brother's eye, but pay no attention to the log in your own eye? How can you say to your brother, 'Please, brother, let me take that speck out of your eye,' yet cannot even see the log in your own eye? You hypocrite! First take the log out of your own eye, and then you will be able to see clearly to take the speck out of your brother's eye.

"Do not give what is holy to dogs - they will only turn and attack you.

Do not throw your pearls in front of pigs - they will only trample them underfoot."

68 Ask, Seek and Knock

Matthew 7:7-12; Luke 11:9-13

"Ask, and you will receive; seek, and you will find; knock, and the door will be opened to you.

"For everyone who asks will receive, and anyone who seeks will find, and the door will be opened to those who knock.

"Would any of you who are fathers give your son a stone when he asks for bread? Or would you give him a snake when he asks for a fish? Or would you give him a scorpion when he asks for an egg? As bad as you are, you know how to give good things to your children. How much more, then, will the Father in heaven give the Holy Spirit and good things to those who ask Him!"

69 Narrow Gate

Matthew 7:13-14; 21-23; Luke 13:22-33

Someone asked him, "Sir, will just a few people be saved?"

Jesus answered them, "Go in through the narrow gate because the gate to hell is wide and the road that leads to it is easy, and there are many who travel it. But the gate to life is narrow and the way that leads to it is hard, and there are few people who find it. Many people will surely try to go in but will not be able.

"The master of the house will get up and close the gate; then when you stand outside and begin to knock on the gate and say, 'Open the gate for us, sir!' he will answer you, 'I don't know where you come from!' Then you will answer, 'We ate and drank with you; you taught in our town!'

"Not everyone who calls me, 'Lord, Lord' will enter into the Kingdom of heaven, but only those who do what my Father in heaven wants them to do. When the Judgment Day comes, many will say to me, 'Lord, Lord! In your name we spoke God's message, by your name we drove out many demons and performed many miracles!' Then will I say to them, 'I never knew you. Get away from me, you wicked people!'

"How you will cry and gnash your teeth when you see Abraham, Isaac and Jacob and all the prophets in the Kingdom of God, while you are thrown out!

" People will come from the east and the west, from the north and the south, and sit at the feast in the Kingdom of God. Then those who are now last will be first, and those who are now first will be last."

At that same time some Pharisees came to Jesus and said to him, "You must get out of here and go somewhere else, because Herod wants to kill you."

Jesus answered them, "Go and tell that fox: 'I am driving out demons and performing cures today and tomorrow, and on the third day I shall finish my work.'

"Yet I must be on my way today, tomorrow, and the next day; it is not right for a prophet to be killed anywhere except in Jerusalem."

70 A Tree and Its Fruit

Matthew 7:15-20; 12:33-37; Luke 6:43-45

"Be on your guard against false prophets; they come to you looking like sheep on the outside, but on the inside they are really like wild wolves. You will know them by what they do. Thorn bushes do not bear grapes, and briers do not bear figs.

"A healthy tree bears good fruit; but a poor tree bears bad fruit. A healthy tree cannot bear bad fruit, and a poor tree cannot bear good fruit. A tree is known by the kind of fruit it bears. And any tree that does not bear good fruit is cut down and thrown in the fire.

"You snakes - how can you say good things when you are evil? For the mouth speaks what the heart is full of. A good person brings good things out of a treasure of good things; a bad person brings bad things out of a treasure of bad things. So, then, you will know the false prophets by what they do.

"You can be sure that on the Judgment Day you will have to give account of every useless word you have ever spoken. Your words will be used to judge you - to declare you either innocent or guilty."

71 Two House Builders

Matthew 7:24-8:1; Luke 6:46-7:1a

"Why do you call me, 'Lord, Lord,' and yet don't do what I tell you? Anyone who comes to me and listens to my words and obeys them. I will show you what he is like.

"He is like a wise man who, in building his house, dug deep and laid the foundation on rock. The rain poured down, the rivers flooded over, and the wind blew hard against that house but could not shake it, because it was well built on the rock.

"But anyone who hears my words and does not obey them is like a foolish man who built his house on sand without laying a foundation. The rain poured down, the rivers flooded over, and the wind blew hard against that house.

"When the flood hit that house it fell at once - and what a terrible crash that was!"

When Jesus finished saying these things, the crowd was amazed at the way he taught. He wasn't like the teachers of the Law; instead, he taught with authority.

When Jesus came down from the hill, large crowds followed him.

He went to Capernaum.

IV. LATER GALILEAN MINISTRY

The Later Galilean Ministry, a period of ten months, covers the period from the Sermon on the Mount to the feeding of the five thousand and involves four journeys:

From Capernaum to Nain through southern Galilee and return
From Capernaum to Gerasa and return
From Capernaum to Nazareth through central Galilee and return
From Capernaum to Bethsaida and return

72 Jesus Heals Roman Officer's Servant

Matthew 8:5-13; Luke 7:1b-10

Jesus entered Capernaum. A Roman officer there had a servant who was very dear to him; the man was sick and about to die. When the officer heard about Jesus, he sent some Jewish elders to ask him to come and heal his servant. They came to Jesus and begged him earnestly, "This man really deserves your help. He loves our people and he himself built a synagogue for us. His servant is sick in bed at home, unable to move and suffering terribly.

"I will go and make him well," Jesus said.

So Jesus went with them. He was not far from the house when the officer sent friends to tell him, "Sir, don't trouble yourself. I do not deserve to have you come into my house, neither do I consider myself worthy to come to you in person. Just give the order, and my servant will get well. I, too, am a man placed under the authority of superior officers, and I have soldiers under me. I order this one, 'Go!' and he goes; I order that one, 'Come!' and he comes; and I order my slave, 'Do this!' and he does it."

When Jesus heard this, he was surprised and said to the people following him, "I tell you, I have never found anyone in Israel with faith like this. I assure you that many will come from the east and the west and sit down with Abraham, Isaac, and Jacob at the feast in the Kingdom of heaven. But those who should be in the Kingdom will be thrown out into the darkness, where they will cry and gnash their teeth." Then Jesus said, "Go home, and what you believe will be done for you."

And the officer's servant was healed that very moment.

The messengers went back to the officer's house and found his servant well.

Insight: *First journey - From Capernaum to Nain through Southern Galilee and return.*

73 Jesus Raises a Widow's Son

Luke 7:11-17

Soon afterward Jesus went to a town named Nain, accompanied by his disciples and a large crowd. Just as he arrived at the gate of the town, a funeral procession was coming out. The dead man was the only son of a woman who was a widow, and a large crowd from the town was with her. When the Lord saw her, his heart was filled with pity for her, and he said to her, "Don't cry. " Then he walked over and touched the coffin, and the men carrying it stopped. Jesus said, "Young man! Get up, I tell you!" The dead man sat up and began to talk, and Jesus gave him back to his mother.

They were all filled with fear and praised God. "A great prophet has appeared among us!" they said; "God has come to save his people!"

This news about Jesus went out through all the country and the surrounding territory.

74 Messengers from John the Baptist

Matthew 11:2-19; Luke 7:18-35

When John's disciples told him, in prison, about all the things that Christ was doing, he called two of them and sent them to the Lord to ask him, "Are you the one John said was going to come, or should we expect someone else?"

When they came to Jesus they said, "John the Baptist sent us to ask if you are the one he said was going to come, or should we expect someone else?"

At that very time Jesus healed many people from their sicknesses, diseases, and evil spirits, and gave sight to many blind people. He answered John's messengers, "Go back and tell John what you have seen and heard: the blind can see, the lame can walk, those who suffer from dreaded skin diseases are made clean, the deaf hear, the dead are brought back to life, and the Good News is preached to the poor. How happy are those who have no doubts about me!"

After John's messengers had left, Jesus began to speak about him to the crowds: "When you went out to John in the desert, what did you expect to see? A blade of grass bending in the wind? What did you go out to see? A man dressed up in fancy clothes? People who dress like that and live in luxury are found in palaces! Tell me, what did you go out to see? A prophet? Yes indeed, but you saw much more than a prophet. For John is the one of whom the scripture says: 'God said, I will send my messenger ahead of you to open the way for you.' I tell you," Jesus added, "John is greater than anyone who has ever lived. But the one who is least in the Kingdom of God is greater than John.

"From the time John preached his message until this very day the Kingdom of heaven has suffered violent attacks, and violent men try to seize it.

Until the time of John all the prophets and the Law of Moses spoke about the Kingdom; and if you are willing to believe their message, John is Elijah, whose coming was predicted. Listen, then, if you have ears!"

All the people heard him; they, and especially the tax collectors, were the ones who had obeyed God's righteous demands and had been baptized by John. But the Pharisees and the teachers of the Law rejected God's purpose for themselves and refused to be baptized by John.

Jesus continued, "Now, to what can I compare the people of this day? What are they like? They are like children sitting in the marketplace.

"One group shouts to the other, 'We played wedding music for you, but you wouldn't dance! We sang funeral songs, but you wouldn't cry! John the Baptist came, and he fasted and drank no wine, and you said, 'He has a demon in him!' The Son of Man came, and he ate and drank, and you said, 'Look at this man! He is a glutton and wine drinker, a friend of tax collectors and outcasts!'

"God's wisdom, however, is shown to be true by all who accept it by its results)."

75 Women Who Accompanied Jesus

Luke 8:1-3

Sometime later Jesus travelled through towns and villages, preaching the Good News about the Kingdom of God. The twelve disciples went with him, and so did some women who had been healed of evil spirits and diseases: Mary (who was called Magdalene), from whom seven demons had been driven out; Joanna whose husband Chuza was an officer in Herod's court; and Susanna, and many other women who used their own resources to help Jesus and his disciples.

76 Jesus and Beelzebul

Matthew 12:22-32; Mark 3:22-30; Luke 11:14-23

Then some people brought to Jesus a man who was blind and could not talk because he had a demon. Jesus healed the man, so that he was able to talk and see. The crowds were all amazed at what Jesus had done. "Could he be the Son of David?" they asked.

When the Pharisees and some teachers of the Law who had come from Jerusalem heard this, they replied, "He has Beelzebul in him! He drives out demons only because their ruler Beelzebul gives him power to do so."

Others wanted to trap Jesus, so they asked him to perform a miracle to show God approved of him. But Jesus knew what they were thinking, so Jesus called them to him and spoke to them in parables.

"How can Satan drive out Satan? Any country that divides itself into groups which fight each other will not last very long; a family divided against itself falls apart, so if Satan's kingdom has groups fighting each other, how can it last? It cannot last, but will fall apart and come to an end. You say that I drive out demons because Beelzebul gives me the power to do so.

"If this is how I drive them out, how do your followers drive them out?

"Your own followers prove that you are wrong! No, it is rather by God's power (Spirit) that I drive out demons, and this proves that the Kingdom of God has already come to you.

"When a strong man, with all his weapons ready, guards his own house, all his belongings are safe. No one can break into a strong man's house and take away his belongings unless he first ties up the strong man; then he can plunder his house. But when a stronger man attacks him and defeats him, he carries away all the weapons the owner was depending on and divides up what he stole.

"Anyone who is not for me is really against me; anyone who does not help me gather is really scattering. For this reason I tell you: people can be forgiven any sin and any evil thing they say; but whoever says evil things against the Holy Spirit will not be forgiven. Anyone who says something against the Son of Man can be forgiven; but whoever says something against the Holy Spirit will not be forgiven - now or ever, because he has committed an eternal sin." (Jesus said this because some people were saying, "He has an evil spirit in him.")

77 Return of the Evil Spirit

Matthew 12:43-45; Luke 11:24-28

"When an evil spirit goes out of a person, it travels over dry country looking for a place to rest. If it can't find one, it says to itself, 'I will go back to my house.' So it goes back and finds the house empty, clean, and all fixed up. Then it goes out and brings along seven other spirits even worse than itself, and they come and live there. So when it is all over, that person is in worse shape than at the beginning. This is what will happen to the evil people of this day."

When Jesus had said this, a woman spoke up from the crowd and said to him, "How happy is the woman who bore you and nursed you!"

But Jesus answered, "Rather, how happy are those who hear the word of God and obey it!"

78 Demand for a Miracle

Matthew 12:38-42; Luke 11:29-32

Then some teachers of the Law and some Pharisees spoke up. "Teacher, " they said, "we want to see you perform a miracle."

"How evil and godless are the people of this day!" Jesus exclaimed. "You ask me for a miracle? No! The only miracle you will be given is the miracle of the prophet Jonah. In the same way that the prophet Jonah spent three days and nights in the big fish, a sign for the people of this day, so will the Son of Man spend three days and nights in the depths of the earth.

"On the Judgment Day the people of Nineveh will stand up and accuse you, because they turned from their sins when they heard Jonah preach; and I tell you that there is something here greater than Jonah!

"On the Judgment Day the Queen of Sheba will stand up and accuse you, because she travelled all the way from her country to listen to King Solomon's wise teaching; and I assure you that there is something here greater than Solomon!"

79 Jesus' Mother and Brothers

Matthew 12:46-50; Mark 3:20-21; Mark 3:31-35; Luke 8:19-21

Then Jesus went home. Again such a large crowd gathered that Jesus and his disciples had no time to eat. When his family heard about it, they set out to take charge of him, because people were saying," He's gone mad!"

Jesus was still talking to the people when his mother and brothers arrived but were unable to join him because of the crowd. They stood outside the house and sent in a message, asking to speak with him. A crowd was sitting around Jesus. One of the people there said to him, "Look, your mother and brothers and sisters are standing outside, and they want to speak with you."

Jesus answered, "Who is my mother? Who are my brothers?" Then he pointed to his disciples and said, "Look. Here are my mother and my brothers! Whoever does what my Father in heaven wants is my brother, my sister, and my mother. My mother and brothers are those who hear the word of God and obey it."

80 Parable of the Sower

Matthew13:1-9; Mark 4:1-9; Luke 8:4-8

That same day Jesus left the house and went to the lakeside, where he sat down to teach. The crowd that gathered around him was so large that he got into a boat and sat in it. The boat was out in the water, and the crowd stood on the shore at the water's edge.

"He used parables to teach them many things, saying to them: "Listen! Once there was a man who went out to sow grain. As he scattered the seed in the field, some of it fell along the path, where it was stepped on, and the birds ate it up. Some of it fell on rocky ground, where there was little soil.

"The seeds soon sprouted, because the soil wasn't deep. But when the sun came up, it burned the young plants; and because the soil had no moisture, the roots had not grown deep enough, and the plants soon dried up.

"Some of the seed fell among thorn bushes, which grew up and choked the plants, and they didn't bear grain.

"But some seeds fell in good soil, and the plants sprouted, grew, and bore grain: some had thirty grains, others sixty, and others one hundred."

And Jesus concluded, "Listen, then, if you have ears!"

81 Purpose of the Parables

Matthew 13:10-17; Mark 4:10-12; Luke 8:9-10

When Jesus was alone, some of those who had heard him came to him with the twelve disciples and asked him, "Why do you use parables when you talk to the people?"

Jesus answered, "The knowledge of the secrets of the Kingdom of heaven has been given to you, but not to them. But the others, who are on the outside, hear all things by means of parables. For the person who has something will be given more, so that he will have more than enough, but the person who has nothing will have taken away from him even the little he has. The reason I use parables in talking to them is that they look, but do not see, and they listen, but do not hear or understand. So the prophecy of Isaiah applies to them:

'This people will listen and listen, but not understand;
they will look and look, but not see,
because their minds are dull,
and they have stopped up their ears
and have closed their eyes.

Otherwise, their eyes would see,
their ears would hear,
their minds would understand,
and they would turn to me, says God,
and I would heal them.'
FP Isaiah 6:9-10

"As for you, how fortunate you are! Your eyes see and your ears hear. I assure you that many prophets and many of God's people wanted very much to see what you see, but they could not, and to hear what you hear, but they did not."

82 Jesus Explains the Parable of the Sower

Matthew 13:18-23; Mark 4:13-20; Luke 8:11-15

Then Jesus asked them, "Don't you understand this parable? How, then, will you ever understand any parable? Listen, then, and learn what the parable of the sower means.

"The seed is the word of God. The sower sows God's message. Some people are like the seeds that fall along the path. The seeds that fell along the path stand for those who hear the message about the Kingdom but do not understand it; as soon as they hear the message Satan, the Evil One, comes and snatches away what was sown in their hearts in order to keep them from believing and being saved.

"Other people are like the seeds that fall on rocky ground. As soon as they hear the message, they receive it gladly.

"But it does not sink deep into them, and they don't last long. They believe only for a while but when the time of testing comes, they fall away. So when trouble or persecution comes because of the message, they give up at once.

"Other people are like the seeds sown among the thorn bushes. These are the ones who hear the message, but the worries about this life, the love for riches, and all other kinds of desires crowd in and choke the message, and they don't bear fruit, their fruit never ripens.

"But other people are like seeds sown in good soil. They hear the message, accept it, and retain it in a good and obedient heart, and they persist until they bear fruit: some thirty, some sixty, and some one hundred."

83 A Lamp Under a Bowl

Mark 4:21-25; Luke 8:16-18

Jesus continued, "Does anyone ever bring in a lamp and put it under a bowl or under the bed? Instead, it is put on the lamp stand, so that people will see the light as they come in.

"Whatever is hidden away will be brought out into the open, and whatever is covered up will be found and brought to light.

"Listen, then, if you have ears!"

He also said to them, "Pay attention to what you hear! The same rules you use to judge others will be used by God to judge you - but with even greater severity. Those who have something will be given more, and those who have nothing will have taken away from them even the little they have."

84 Parable of the Growing Seed

Mark 4:26-29

Jesus went on to say, "The Kingdom of God is like this. A man scatters seed in his field. He sleeps at night, is up and about during the day, and all the while the seeds are sprouting and growing.

"Yet he does not know how it happens.

"The soil itself makes the plants grow and bear fruit; first the tender stalk appears, then the head, and finally the head full of grain. When the grain is ripe, the man starts cutting it with his sickle, because harvest time has come."

85 Parable of the Weeds

Matthew 13:24-30

Jesus told them another parable: "The Kingdom of heaven is like this. A man sowed good seed in his field. One night, when everyone was asleep, an enemy came and sowed weeds among the wheat and went away. When the plants grew and the heads of grain began to form, then the weeds showed up.

The man's servants came to him and said, 'Sir, it was good seed you sowed in your field; where did the weeds come from?'

'It was some enemy who did this,' he answered.

'Do you want us to go and pull up the weeds?' they asked him.

'No,' he answered, 'because as you gather the weeds you might pull up some of the wheat along with them. Let the wheat and the weeds both grow together until harvest. Then I will tell the harvest workers to pull up the weeds first, tie them in bundles and burn them, and then to gather in the wheat and put it in my barn.'"

86 Parable of the Mustard Seed

Matthew 13:31-32; Mark 4:30-32; Luke 13:18-19

Jesus told them another parable. "What shall we say the Kingdom of God is like?" asked Jesus.

"What parable shall we use to explain it? It is like this. A man takes a mustard seed, the smallest seed in the world, and plants it in the ground. After a while it grows up and becomes a tree, the biggest of all plants. It puts out such large branches that the birds come and make their nests in its shade (branches)."

87 Parable of the Yeast

Matthew13:33; Luke 13:20-21

Jesus told them still another parable:

Again Jesus asked, "What shall I compare the Kingdom of God with? It is like this. A woman takes some yeast and mixes it with a bushel of flour until the whole batch of dough rises."

88 Jesus' Use of Parables

Matthew 13:34-35; Mark 4:33-34

Jesus preached his message to the people, using many other parables like these; he told them as much as they could understand.

He would not speak to them without using parables, but when he was alone with his disciples he would explain everything to them. He did this to make come true what the prophet had said,

> "I will use parables when I speak to them; I will tell them things unknown since the creation of the world." FP Psalm78:2

89 Jesus Explains the Parable of the Weeds

Matthew 13:36-43

When Jesus had left the crowd and gone indoors, his disciples came to him and said, "Tell us what the parable of the weeds in the field means."

Jesus answered, "The man who sowed the good seed is the Son of Man; the field is the world; the good seed is the people who belong to the Kingdom; the weeds are the people who belong to the Evil One; and the enemy who sowed the weeds is the Devil.

"The harvest is the end of the age, and the harvest workers are angels.

"Just as the weeds are gathered up and burned in the fire, so the same thing will happen at the end of the age: the Son of Man will send out his angels to gather up out of his Kingdom all those who cause people to sin and all others who do evil things, and they will throw them into the fiery furnace, where they will cry and gnash their teeth.

"Then God's people will shine like the sun in their Father's Kingdom. Listen, then, if you have ears!"

90 Parable of the Hidden Treasure

Matthew 13:34

"The Kingdom of heaven is like this. A man happens to find a treasure hidden in a field. He covers it up again, and he is so happy that he goes and sells everything he has, and then goes back and buys that field."

91 Parable of the Pearl

Matthew 13:45-46

"Also, the Kingdom of heaven is like this. A man is looking for fine pearls, and when he finds one that is unusually fine, he goes and sells everything he has, and buys that pearl."

92 Parable of the Net

Matthew 13:47-50

"Also, the Kingdom of heaven is like this. Some fishermen throw their net out in the lake and catch all kinds of fish. When the net is full, they pull it to shore and sit down to divide the fish: the good ones go into the buckets, the worthless ones are thrown away. It will be like this at the end of the age: the angels will go out and gather up the evil people from among the good and will throw them into the fiery furnace, where they will cry and gnash their teeth.

"Do you understand these things?" Jesus asked them.

"Yes," they answered.

93 New and Old Truths

Matthew 13:51-53

So he replied, "This means, then, that every teacher of the Law who becomes a disciple in the Kingdom of heaven is like a homeowner who takes new and old things out of his storage room."

When Jesus finished telling them these parables, he left that place.

94 Would-be Followers of Jesus

Matthew 8:18-22; Luke 9:57-62

A teacher of the Law came to him. "Teacher," he said, "I am ready to go with you wherever you go."

Jesus answered him, "Foxes have holes, and birds have nests, but the Son of Man has no place to lie down and rest."

He said to another man, who was a disciple, "Follow me."

But that man said, "Sir, first let me go back and bury my father."

Jesus answered, "Let the dead bury their own dead. You go and proclaim the Kingdom of God."

Someone else said, "I will follow you, sir; but first let me go and say good-bye to my family."

Jesus said to him, "Anyone who starts to plow and then keeps looking back is of no use for the Kingdom of God."

95 Jesus Calms a Storm

Matthew 8:23-27; Mark 4:35-41; Luke 8:22-25

On the evening of that same day Jesus said to his disciples, "Let us go across to the other side of the lake." So they left the crowd; the disciples got into the boat in which Jesus was already sitting, and took him with them. Other boats were there too.

Suddenly a fierce storm hit the lake. A strong wind blew down on the lake, the waves began to spill over into the boat, so that it was about to fill with water. They were all in great danger. Jesus was in the back of the boat, sleeping with his head on a pillow. The disciples went to Jesus and woke him up saying, "Master, Master! Don't you care that we are about to die?"

Jesus stood up and commanded the wind, "Be quiet!" and he said to the waves, "Be still!" The wind died down, and there was a great calm.

Then Jesus said to his disciples, "Why are you so frightened? Do you still have no faith?"

But they were amazed and terribly afraid, and began to say to one another, "Who is this man? Even the wind and the waves obey him!"

Insight: *Second Journey - From Capernaum to Gerasa and return.*

96 Jesus Heals Men with Demons

Matthew 28-34; Mark 5:1-20; Luke 8:26-39

Jesus and his disciples arrived on the other side of Lake Galilee, in the territory of Gerasa (Gadara).

Jesus stepped ashore and was met by two men who came out of the burial caves there.

> ***Insight:*** *Matthew states that there were two men with demons who were healed on this occasion. Mark and Luke only tell the story of one of the men.*

These men were so fierce that no one dared travel on that road. For a long time one of the men had gone without clothes and would not stay at home, but spent his time in the burial caves and lived among the tombs.

Even though he was kept a prisoner, nobody could keep him tied with chains anymore; many times his feet and hands had been tied, but every time he broke the chains and smashed the irons on his feet. He was too strong for anyone to control him. Day and night he wandered among the tombs and through the hills, driven by the demon out into the desert, screaming and cutting himself with stones.

He was some distance away when he saw Jesus; so he ran, fell on his knees before him, and screamed in a loud voice, "Jesus, Son of the Most High God! What do you want with me? For God's sake, I beg you, don't punish me!" (He said this because Jesus was saying, "Evil spirit, come out of this man!")

So Jesus asked him, "What is your name?"

The man answered, "My name is 'Mob'; there are so many of us!" And he kept begging Jesus not to send the evil spirits out of that region into the abyss.

There was a large herd of pigs nearby, feeding on a hillside. So the spirits begged Jesus, "If you are going to drive us out, send us into that herd of pigs, and let us go into them."

"Go," Jesus told them, and the evil spirits went out of the men and entered the pigs. The whole herd - about two thousand pigs in all - rushed down the side of the cliff into the lake and was drowned.

The men who had been taking care of the pigs saw what happened, so they ran off and spread the news in the town and among the farms. People went out to see what had happened, and when they came to Jesus, they found the men from whom the demons had gone out sitting at the feet of Jesus, clothed and in their right mind; and they were all afraid. Those who had seen it told the people how the men had been cured.

Then all the people from that territory asked Jesus to go away, because they were terribly afraid.

As Jesus was getting into the boat, one of the men who had had the demons begged him, "Let me go with you!"

But Jesus would not let him. Instead, he told him, "Go back home to your family and tell them how much the Lord has done for you and how kind he has been to you."

So the man left and went all through the Ten Towns telling what Jesus had done for him. And all who heard it were amazed.

97 Jairus' Daughter and Woman Who Touched Jesus' Cloak

Matthew 9:18-26; Mark 5:21-43; Luke 8:40-56

When Jesus returned to the other side of the lake, the people welcomed him, because they had all been waiting for him. Then a man named Jairus arrived; he was an official in the local synagogue. He threw himself down at Jesus' feet and begged him earnestly to go to his home, "My little daughter is very sick. Please come and place your hands on her, so that she will get well and live!" His only daughter, who was twelve years old, was dying.

So Jesus got up and followed him, and his disciples went along with him. So many people were going along with him that they were crowding him from every side.

There was a woman who had suffered terribly from severe bleeding for twelve years, even though she had been treated by many doctors. She had spent all her money, but instead of getting better she got worse all the time. She had heard about Jesus, so she came in the crowd behind him, saying to herself, "If I touch just his clothes, I will get well."

She touched his cloak and her bleeding stopped at once; and she had the feeling inside herself that she was healed of her trouble. At once Jesus knew that power had gone out of him, so he turned around in the crowd and asked, "Who touched my clothes?"

Everyone denied it, and Peter said, "Master, the people are all around you and crowding in on you; why do you ask who touched you?"

But Jesus said, "Someone touched me, for I knew it when power went out of me." Jesus kept looking round to see who had done it. The woman saw that she had been found out, so she came, trembling with fear, and threw herself at Jesus' feet. There in front of everybody, she told him why she had touched him and how she had been healed at once.

Jesus said to her, "My daughter, your faith has made you well. Go in peace, and be healed from your trouble."

While Jesus was saying this, some messengers came from Jairus's house and told him, "Your daughter has died. Why bother the Teacher any longer?"

Jesus paid no attention to what they said, but told Jairus, "Don't be afraid, only believe, and she will be well."

When he arrived at the house, everyone there was crying and mourning for the child. Jesus saw the confusion and heard all the loud crying and wailing.

When he saw the musicians for the funeral and the people all stirred up, he went in and said to them,

"Get out everybody! Why all this confusion? Why are you crying? The child is not dead? she is only sleeping!"

They started making fun of him, because they knew that she was dead, so he put them all out, took the child's father and mother, and his three disciples, and went into the room where the child was lying. He took her by the hand and said to her, "Talitha, koum," which means, "Little girl, I tell you to get up!"

Her life returned and she got up at once and started walking around. Jesus ordered them to give her something to eat. Her parents were astounded, but Jesus commanded them not to tell anyone what had happened.

98 Jesus Heals Two Blind Men

Matthew 9:27-31

Jesus left that place, and as he walked along two blind men started following him. "Have mercy on us, Son of David!" they shouted.

When Jesus had gone indoors, the two blind men came to him, and he asked them, "Do you believe that I can heal you?"

"Yes, sir!" they answered.

Then Jesus touched their eyes and said, "Let it happen, then, just as you believe!" and their sight was restored. Jesus spoke sternly to them, "Don't tell this to anyone!"

But they left and spread the news about Jesus all over that part of the country.

99 Jesus Heals a Dumb Man

Matthew 9:32-34

As the men were leaving, some people brought to Jesus a man who could not talk because he had a demon. But as soon as the demon was driven out, the man started talking, and everyone was amazed. "We have never seen anything like this in Israel!" they exclaimed.

But the Pharisees said, "It is the chief of the demons who gives Jesus the power to drive out demons."

Insight: *Third journey - From Capernaum to Nazareth through Central Galilee and return.*

100 Jesus Has Pity for People

Matthew 9:35-38

So Jesus went round visiting all the towns and villages. He taught in their synagogues, preached the Good News of the Kingdom, and healed people with every kind of disease and sickness.

As he saw the crowds, his heart was filled with pity for them, because they were worried and helpless, like sheep without a shepherd. So he said to his disciples, "The harvest is large, but there are few workers to gather it in. Pray to the owner of the harvest that he will send out workers to gather in his harvest."

101 The Mission of the Twelve

Matthew 10:5-15; Mark 6:6b-13; Luke 9:1-6

Jesus taught in all the neighboring villages. Then he called together his twelve apostles and sent them out two by two and gave them power and authority to drive out all demons and to cure diseases.

"As you go, announce that the kingdom of heaven will soon be here. Stay away from the Gentiles and don't go to any Samaritan town.

"Go only to the people of Israel because they are like a flock of lost sheep. As you go announce that the kingdom of heaven will soon be here! Heal the sick, bring the dead back to life, heal those who suffer from dreaded skin diseases, and drive out demons.

"You received without paying, so give without being paid. You may take along a walking stick. But don't carry food or a traveling bag or any money. It's all right to wear sandals, but don't take along a change of clothes. Workers deserve their food.

"But when you go to a town or village, find someone worthy enough to have you as their guest and stay with them until you leave. When you go into a home, give it your blessing of peace. If the home is deserving, let your blessing remain with them. But if the home isn't deserving, take back your blessing of peace. If someone won't welcome you or listen to your message, leave their home or town.

"And shake the dust from your feet at them as a warning to them. I promise you that the day of judgment will be easier for the towns of Sodom and Gomorrah than for that town."

The apostles left and started telling everyone to turn to God. They forced out many demons and healed a lot of sick people by putting olive oil on them.

102 Jesus Sends out Seventy-two

Luke 10:1-12

After this the Lord chose another seventy-two men and sent them out two by two, to go ahead of him to every town and place where he himself was about to go.

He said to them, "There is a large harvest, but few workers to gather it in. Pray to the owner of the harvest that he will send out workers to gather in his harvest.

"Go! I am sending you like lambs among wolves. Don't take a purse or a beggar's bag or shoes; don't stop to greet anyone on the road. Whenever you go into a house, first say, 'Peace be with this house.' If someone who is peace-loving lives there, let your greeting of peace remain on that person; if not, take back your greeting of peace. Stay in that same house, eating and drinking what they offer you, for workers should be given their pay.

"Don't move around from one house to another. Whenever you go into a town and are made welcome, eat what is set before you, heal the sick in that town, and say to the people there, 'The Kingdom of God has come near you.'

"But whenever you go into a town and are not welcomed, go out in the streets and say, 'Even the dust from your town that sticks to our feet we wipe off against you.' But remember that on the Judgment Day God will show more mercy to Sodom than to that town!"

103 Unbelieving Towns

Matthew 11:20-24; Luke 10:13-16

The people in the towns where Jesus had performed most of his miracles did not turn from their sins, so he reproached those towns. "How terrible it will be for you, Chorazin! How terrible for you too, Bethsaida! If the miracles which were performed in you had been performed in Tyre and Sidon, the people there would have long ago put on sackcloth, and sprinkled ashes on themselves, to show that they had turned from their sins!

"I assure you that on the Judgment Day God will show more mercy to the people of Tyre and Sidon than to you! And as for you, Capernaum! Did you want to lift yourself up to heaven? You will be thrown down to hell! If the miracles which were performed in you had been performed in Sodom, it would still be in existence today! You can be sure that on the Judgment Day God will show more mercy to Sodom than to you!"

Jesus said to his disciples. "Whoever listens to you listens to me; whoever rejects you rejects me; and whoever rejects me rejects the one who sent me."

104 Return of the Seventy-two

Luke 10:17-20

The seventy-two men came back in great joy. "Lord," they said, "even the demons obeyed us when we gave them a command in your name!"

Jesus answered them, "I saw Satan fall like lightning from heaven. Listen! I have given you authority, so that you can walk on snakes and scorpions, and overcome all the power of the enemy, and nothing will hurt you.

"But don't be glad because the evil spirits obey you; rather be glad because your names are written in heaven."

105 Jesus Rejoices

Matthew 11:25-30; Luke 10:21-24

At that time Jesus was filled with joy by the Holy Spirit and said, "Father, Lord of Heaven and earth! I thank you because you have shown to the unlearned what you have hidden from the wise and learned. Yes, Father, this was how you were pleased to have it happen.

"My Father has given me all things. No one knows who the Son is except the Father, and no one knows who the Father is except the Son and those to whom the Son chooses to reveal him.

"Come to me, all of you who are tired from carrying heavy loads, and I will give you rest. Take my yoke and put it on you, and learn from me, because I am gentle and humble in spirit; and you will find rest. For the yoke I will give you is easy, and the load I will put on you is light."

Then Jesus turned to the disciples and said to them privately, "How fortunate you are to see the things you see! I tell you that many prophets and kings wanted to see what you see, but they could not, and to hear what you hear, but they did not."

106 Coming Persecutions

Matthew 10:16-25; Luke 12:11-12

"Listen! I am sending you out just like sheep to a pack of wolves. You must be as cautious as snakes and as gentle as doves. Watch out, for there will be those men who will arrest you and take you to court, and they will whip you in the synagogues.

"For my sake you will be brought to trial before rulers and kings, to tell the Good News to them and to the Gentiles. When they bring you to trial, do not worry about what you are going to say or how you will say it; when the time comes, you will be given what you will say. For the words you speak will not be yours; they will come from the Spirit of your Father speaking through you. For the Holy Spirit will teach you at that time what you should say.

"People will hand over their own brothers to be put to death, and fathers will do the same to their children; children will turn against their parents and have them put to death. Everyone will hate you because of me. But whoever holds out to the end will be saved. When they persecute you in one town, run away to another one. I assure you that you will not finish your work in all the towns of Israel before the Son of Man comes.

"No pupil is greater than his teacher; no slave is greater than his master. So a pupil should be satisfied to become like his teacher, and a slave like his master. If the head of the family is called Beelzebul, the members of the family will be called even worse names!"

107 Whom to Fear

Matthew 10:26-31; Luke 12:4-7

"So do not be afraid of people. What is now covered up will be uncovered, and every secret will be made known. What I am telling you in the dark you must repeat in broad daylight, and what you have heard in private you must announce from the housetops. Do not be afraid of those who can kill the body but cannot afterward do anything worse - cannot kill the soul. I will show you whom to fear; rather be afraid of God, who can destroy both body and soul in hell. Believe me, he is the one you must fear!

"For only a penny you can buy two sparrows. Aren't five sparrows sold for two pennies? Yet not one sparrow falls to the ground without your Father's consent. As for you, even the hairs of your head have all been counted. So do not be afraid; you are worth much more than many sparrows."

108 Confessing and Rejecting Christ

Matthew 10:32-33; Luke 12:8-10

"I assure you that whoever declares publicly that he belongs to me, the Son of Man will do the same for them before the angels of God and before my Father in heaven. But those who reject me publicly, the Son of Man will also reject them before the angels of God and before my Father in heaven.

"Anyone who says a word against the Son of Man can be forgiven; but whoever says evil things against the Holy Spirit will not be forgiven."

109 Cost of Being a Disciple

Matthew 10:34-39; Luke 12:49-53; 14:25-33

Once when large crowds of people were going along with Jesus, he turned and said to them, "I came to set the earth on fire; and how I wish it were already kindled! I have a baptism to receive, and how distressed I am until it is over! Do not think that I have come to bring peace to the world; no, I did not come to bring peace, but division's sword.

"From now on a family of five will be divided, three against two and two against three. Fathers will be against their sons, and sons against their fathers; mothers will be against their daughters, and daughters against their mothers; mothers-in-law will be against their daughters-in-law, and daughters-in-law will be against their mothers-in-law; your worst enemies will be the members of your own family.

"Those who come to me cannot be my disciples unless they love me more than they love father and mother, wife and children, brothers and sisters, and themselves as well. Those who love their father or mother more than me are not fit to be my disciples; those who love their son or daughter more than me are not fit to be my disciples.

"Those who do not carry their own cross and come after me and follow in my steps is not fit to be my disciple. Those who try to gain their own life will lose it; but those who lose their life for my sake will gain it.

"If one of you is planning to build a tower, you sit down first and figure out what it will cost, to see if you have enough money to finish the job. If you don't, you will not be able to finish the tower after laying the foundation; and all who see what happened will make fun of you. 'You began to build but can't finish the job!' they will say.'

"If a king goes out with ten thousand men to fight another king who comes against him with twenty thousand men, he will sit down first and decide if he is strong enough to face that other king. If he isn't, he will send messengers to meet the other king to ask for terms of peace while he is still a long way off. In the same way," concluded Jesus, "none of you can be my disciple unless you give up everything you have."

110 Rewards and Ministry

Matthew 10:40-11:1 Mark 9:41

"Whoever welcomes you welcomes me; and whoever welcomes me welcomes the one who sent me. Whoever welcomes God's messenger because he is God's messenger, will share in his reward. And whoever welcomes a good man because he is good, will share in his reward. You can be sure that whoever gives even a drink of cold water to one of the least of these my followers because he is my follower and belongs to me, will certainly receive a reward."

Insight: *Fourth Journey--From Capernaum to Bethsaida and return.*

When Jesus finished giving these instructions to his twelve disciples, he left that place and went off to teach and preach in the towns near there.

111 Death of John the Baptist

Matthew 14:1-12; Mark 6:14-29; Luke 9:7-9

At that time Herod, the ruler of Galilee, heard about Jesus, because Jesus' reputation had spread everywhere. He was very confused, because some people were saying that John the Baptist had come back to life! That is why he had this power to perform miracles.

Others were saying that Elijah had appeared, and still others that one of the prophets of long ago had come back to life.

Herod said, "He is really John the Baptist! I had his head cut off, but he has come back to life!" And he kept trying to see Jesus.

Herod himself had ordered John's arrest, and he had him tied up and put in prison. Herod did this because of Herodias, whom he had married, even though she was the wife of his brother Philip. John the Baptist kept telling Herod, "It isn't right for you to marry your brother's wife!"

So Herodias held a grudge against John and wanted to kill him, but she could not because of Herod. Herod was afraid of John because he knew that John was a good and holy man, so he kept him safe. He liked to listen to him, even though he became greatly disturbed every time he heard him.

Herod wanted to kill him, but he was afraid of the Jewish people, because they considered John to be a prophet.

Finally Herodias got her chance. It was on Herod's birthday, when he gave a feast for all the top government officials, the military chiefs, and the leading citizens of Galilee. The daughter of Herodias came in and danced, and pleased Herod and his guests. So the king said to the girl, "What would you like to have? I will give you anything you want." With many vows he said to her, "I swear that I will give you anything you ask for, even as much as half my kingdom!"

So the girl went out and asked her mother, "What shall I ask for?"

"The head of John the Baptist," she answered.

At her mother's suggestion the girl hurried back at once to the king and demanded, "I want you to give me here and now the head of John the Baptist on a plate!"

This made the king very sad, but he could not refuse her because of the vows he had made in front of all his guests. So he sent off a guard at once with orders to bring John's head. The guard left, went to the prison, and cut John's head off; then he brought it on a plate and gave it to the girl, who gave it to her mother. When John's disciples heard about this, they came and got his body and buried it; then they went and told Jesus.

112 Jesus Feeds Five Thousand

Matthew 14:13-21; Mark 6:30-44; Luke 9:10-17; John 6:1-15

The apostles returned and met with Jesus, and told him all they had done and taught.

There were so many people coming and going that Jesus and his disciples didn't even have time to eat.

When Jesus heard the news about John, he said to them, "Let us go off by ourselves to some place where we will be alone and you can rest a while." So they started out in the boat by themselves across Lake Galilee (or, Lake Tiberias, as it is also called) to a lonely place, a town named Bethsaida.

Many people, however, saw them leave and knew at once who they were; so they went from all the towns and ran ahead by land and arrived at the place ahead of Jesus and his disciples.

When Jesus got out of the boat, he saw this large crowd, and his heart was filled with pity for them, because they were like sheep without a shepherd. He welcomed them, spoke to them about the Kingdom of God, and began to teach them many things and healed those who needed it.

That evening, when the sun was beginning to set, Jesus went up a hill and sat down with his disciples. The Passover Festival was near.

When it was getting late his disciples came to him and said, "It is already very late, and this is a lonely place. Send the people away, and let them go to the nearby farms and villages and buy themselves something to eat and find lodging."

"They don't have to leave," answered Jesus. "You yourselves give them something to eat." He asked Philip, "Where can we buy enough food to feed all these people?" (He said this to test Philip; actually he already knew what he would do.) Philip answered, "For everyone to have even a little, it would take more than two hundred silver coins to buy enough bread. Do you want us to go spend two hundred silver coins on bread in order to feed them?"

So Jesus asked them, "How much bread do you have? Go and see."

Another one of his disciples, Andrew, who was Simon Peter's brother, said, "There is a boy here who has five loaves of barley bread and two fish. But they will certainly not be enough for all these people." (There were about five thousand men there, not counting the women and children.)

"Then bring them here to me," Jesus said to his disciples. "Make the people sit down in groups of about fifty each." (There was a lot of grass there.) So the people sat down in rows, in groups of a hundred and groups of fifty. Then Jesus took the five loaves and the two fish, looked up to heaven, and gave thanks to God. He broke the loaves and gave them to his disciples to distribute to the people. He also divided the two fish among them all.

They all had as much as they wanted. When they were all full, he said to his disciples, "Gather the pieces left over; let us not waste a bit." So they gathered them all, and filled twelve baskets with the pieces left over from the five barley loaves which the people had eaten.

Seeing this miracle that Jesus had performed, the people there said, "Surely this is the Prophet who was to come into the world!" Jesus knew that they were about to come and seize him in order to make him king by force; so he went off again to the hills by himself.

113 Jesus Walks on the Water

Matthew 14:22-33; Mark 6:45-52; John 6:16-21

When evening came, Jesus made the disciples get into the boat and go ahead to the other side of the lake toward Capernaum while he sent the people away. After saying good-bye to the people, he went up a hill by himself to pray. Night came on, and Jesus still had not come to them.

Jesus was there alone; and by this time the boat was far out in the lake, about three or four miles, tossed about by the waves, because a strong wind was blowing and stirring up the water. Jesus saw that his disciples were straining against the oars, because they were rowing against the wind; so sometime between three and six o'clock in the morning, he came to them, walking on the water. He was going to pass them by. When they saw him walking on the water they were terrified. "It's a ghost!" they said, and screamed with fear. Jesus spoke to them at once. "Courage!" he said, "It is I. Don't be afraid!"

Then Peter spoke up. "Lord, if it is really you, order me to come out on the water to you."

"Come!" answered Jesus. So Peter got out of the boat and started walking on the water to Jesus. But when he noticed the strong wind, he was afraid and started to sink down in the water. "Save me, Lord!" he cried.

At once Jesus reached out and grabbed hold of him and said, "What little faith you have! Why did you doubt?"

They both got into the boat, and the wind died down, and immediately the boat reached land at the place they were heading for.

The disciples were completely amazed, because they had not understood the real meaning of the feeding of the five thousand; their minds could not grasp it. The disciples in the boat worshiped Jesus. "Truly you are the Son of God!" they exclaimed.

114 Jesus Heals in Gennesaret

Matthew 14:34-36; Mark 6:53-56

They crossed the lake and came to land at Gennesaret, where they tied up the boat. As they left the boat, people recognized Jesus at once. So they ran throughout the whole region; and wherever they heard he was, they brought the sick lying on their mats.

And everywhere Jesus went, to villages, towns, or farms, people would take their sick to the marketplaces and beg him to let the sick at least touch the edge of his cloak. And all who touched it were made well.

115 Teaching of the Ancestors

Matthew 15:1-9; Mark 7:1-13

Some Pharisees and teachers of the Law who had come from Jerusalem gathered around Jesus. They noticed that some of his disciples were eating their food with hands that were ritually unclean - that is, they had not washed them in the way the Pharisees said people should.

(For the Pharisees, as well as the rest of the Jews, follow the teaching they received from their ancestors.

They do not eat unless they wash their hands in the proper way, nor do they eat anything that comes from the market unless they wash it first. And they follow many other rules which they have received, such as the proper way to wash cups, pots, copper bowls, and beds.)

So the Pharisees and the teachers of the Law asked Jesus, "Why is it that your disciples do not follow the teaching handed down by our ancestors, but instead eat with ritually unclean hands?"

Jesus answered, "And why do you disobey God's command and follow your own teaching? You have a clever way of rejecting God's law in order to uphold your own teaching. For God said (and Moses commanded), 'Respect your father and your mother,' and 'If you curse your father or your mother you are to be put to death.'

" But you teach that if a person has something they could use to help their father or mother, but say, 'This belongs to God', they do not need to honor their father. In this way you disregard God's command, in order to follow your own teaching. The teaching you pass on to others cancels out the word of God. And there are many other things like this that you do. You hypocrites! How right Isaiah was when he prophesied about you!"

"These people," says God, "honor me with their words, but their heart is really far away from me. It is no use for them to worship me, because they teach human rules as though they were my laws!"

116 The Things That Make a Person Unclean

Matthew 15:10-20; Mark 7:14-23

Then Jesus called the crowd to him once more and said to them, "Listen to me, all of you, and understand. There is nothing that goes into your mouth from the outside which can make you ritually unclean.

Rather, it is what comes out of you that makes you unclean."

Then the disciples came to him and said, "Do you know that the Pharisees had their feelings hurt by what you said?"

"Every plant which my Father in heaven did not plant will be pulled up," answered Jesus. "Don't worry about them! They are blind leaders of the blind; and when one blind man leads another, both fall into a ditch."

When he left the crowd and went into the house, Peter spoke up, "Explain this saying to us."

Jesus said to them, "You are still no more intelligent than the others. Don't you understand? Nothing that goes into you from the outside can really make you unclean, because anything that goes into your mouth goes into your stomach and then on out of the body." (In saying this, Jesus declared that all foods are fit to be eaten.)

And he went on to say, "But the things that come out of the mouth come from the heart, and these are the things that make you ritually unclean. For from your heart come the evil ideas which lead you to kill, commit adultery, and do other immoral things; to rob, lie, and slander others, be greedy, and do all sorts of evil things; deceit, indecency, jealousy, slander, pride, and folly" - all these evil things come from inside you and make you unclean. But to eat without washing your hands as they say you should - this doesn't make you unclean."

117 The People Seek Jesus

John 6:22-24

Next day the crowd which had stayed on the other side of the lake realized that there had been only one boat there. They knew that Jesus had not gone in it with his disciples, but that they had left without him. Other boats, which were from Tiberias, came to shore near the place where the crowd had eaten the bread after the Lord had given thanks. When the crowd saw that Jesus was not there, nor his disciples, they got into those boats and went to Capernaum, looking for him.

118 Bread of Life

John 6:26-59

When the people found Jesus on the other side of the lake, they said to him, "Teacher, when did you get here?"

Jesus answered, "I am telling you the truth: you are looking for me because you ate the bread and had all you wanted, not because you understood my miracles. Do not work for food that spoils; instead, work for the food that lasts for eternal life. This is the food which the Son of Man will give you, because God, the Father, has put his mark of approval on him."

So they asked him, "What can we do in order to do what God wants us to do?"

Jesus answered, "What God wants you to do is to believe in the One he sent."

They replied, "What miracle will you perform so that we may see it and believe you? What will you do? Our ancestors ate manna in the desert, just as the scripture says, 'He gave them bread from heaven to eat.'"

"I am telling you the truth," Jesus said. "What Moses gave you was not the bread from heaven; it is my Father who gives you the real bread from heaven. For the bread that God gives is he who comes down from heaven and gives life to the world."

"Sir," they asked him, "give us this bread always."

"I am the bread of life," Jesus told them. "Those who come to me will never be hungry; those who believe in me will never be thirsty. Now, I told you that you have seen me but will not believe.

Everyone whom my Father gives me will come to me.

"I will never turn away anyone who comes to me, because I have come down from heaven to do not my own will but the will of him who sent me.

"And it is the will of him who sent me that I should not lose any of all those he has given me, but that I should raise them all to life on the last day. For what my Father wants is that all who see the Son and believe in him should have eternal life. And I will raise them to life on the last day."

The people started grumbling about him, because he said, "I am the bread that came down from heaven." So they said, "This man is Jesus the son of Joseph, isn't he? We know his father and mother. How, then, does he now say he came down from heaven?"

Jesus answered, "Stop grumbling among yourselves. People cannot come to me unless the Father who sent me draws them to me; and I will raise them to life on the last day.

"The prophets wrote, 'Everyone will be taught by God.' Anyone who hears the Father and learns from him comes to me. This does not mean that anyone has seen the Father; he who is from God is the only one who has seen the Father. I am telling you the truth: he who believes has eternal life.

"I am the bread of life. Your ancestors ate the manna in the desert, but they died. But the bread that comes down from heaven is of such a kind that whoever eats it will not die. I am the living bread that came down from heaven. If you eat this bread you will live forever. The bread that I will give you is my flesh, which I give so that the world may live."

This started an angry argument among them. "How can this man give us his flesh to eat?" they asked.

Jesus said to them, "I am telling you the truth: if you do not eat the flesh of the Son of Man and drink his blood, you will not have life in yourselves. Those who eat my flesh and drink my blood have eternal life, and I will raise them to life on the last day. For my flesh is the real food; my blood is the real drink. Those who eat my flesh and drink my blood live in me, and I live in them.

"The living Father sent me, and because of him I live also. In the same way, whoever eats me will live because of me. This, then, is the bread that came down from heaven; it is not like the bread that your ancestors ate, but then later died. The one who eats this bread will live forever."

Jesus said this as he taught in the synagogue in Capernaum.

119 Words of Eternal Life

John 6:60-71

Many of his disciples heard this and said, "This teaching is too hard. Who can listen to it?"

Without being told, Jesus knew that his disciples were grumbling about this, so he said to them, "Does this make you want to give up? Suppose, then, that you should see the Son of Man go back up to the place where he was before? What gives life is God's Spirit; man's power is of no use at all. The words I have spoken to you bring God's life-giving Spirit. Yet some of you do not believe." (Jesus knew from the very beginning who were the ones that would not believe, and which one would betray him.) And he added, "This is the very reason I told you that people cannot come to me unless the Father makes it possible for them to do so."

Because of this, many of Jesus' followers turned back and would not go with him anymore. So he asked the twelve disciples, "And you, would you also like to leave?"

Simon Peter answered him, "Lord, to whom would we go? You have the words that give eternal life. And now we believe and know that you are the Holy One who has come from God."

Jesus replied, "I chose the twelve of you, didn't I? Yet one of you is a devil!" He was talking about Judas, the son of Simon Iscariot. For Judas, even though he was one of the twelve disciples, was going to betray him.

V. MINISTRY IN OTHER REGIONS

The time of retirement, a period of six months, covers the period from just before the feeding of the five thousand to the Feast of Tabernacles and involves one long journey taken in four stages:

From Capernaum to the borders of Tyre and Sidon in Phoenicia
From the borders of Tyre and Sidon to Decapolis
From Decapolis through Dalmanutha and Bethsaida to Caesarea Philippi
From Caesarea Philippi to Capernaum.

Insight: *Jesus' ministry in other regions, a period of six months, covers the period just before the Feeding of the Four Thousand to the Feast of Tabernacles and involves four journeys.*

Insight: *First journey - From Capernaum to the borders of Tyre and Sidon in Phoenicia.*

120 A Woman's Faith

Matthew 15:21-28; Mark 7:24-30

Jesus left that place and went off to the territory near the cities of Tyre and Sidon. He went into a house and did not want anyone to know he was there, but he could not stay hidden. A certain Canaanite woman who lived in that region, whose daughter had an evil spirit in her, heard about Jesus and came to him at once and fell at his feet. The woman was a Gentile, born in the region of Phoenicia of Syria. She begged Jesus to drive the demon out of her daughter. "Son of David!" she cried out. "Have mercy on me, sir! My daughter has a demon and is in a terrible condition."

But Jesus did not say a word to her. His disciples came to him and begged him, "Send her away! She is following us and making all this noise!"

Then Jesus replied, "I have been sent only to those lost sheep of the people of Israel."

At this the woman came and fell at his feet. "Help me, sir!" she said.

Jesus answered, "Let us first feed the children. It isn't right to take the children's food and throw it to the dogs."

"That's true, sir," she answered; "but even the dogs under the table eat the children's leftovers that fall from their master's table."

So Jesus answered her, "You are a woman of great faith! Because of that answer, go back home; what you want will be done for you. You will find that the demon has gone out of your daughter!" And at that very moment her daughter was healed.

She went home and found her child lying on the bed; the demon had indeed gone out of her.

Insight: *Second Journey - From the borders of Tyre and Sidon to the province of Decapolis on the eastern side of Lake Galilee and the Jordan River.*

121 Jesus Heals a Deaf and Dumb Man

Matthew 15:29-31; Mark 7:31-37

Jesus then left the neighborhood of Tyre and went on through Sidon to Lake Galilee, going by way of the territory of the Ten Towns. He climbed a hill and sat down. Large crowds came to him, bringing with them the lame, the blind, the crippled, the dumb, and many other sick people, whom they placed at Jesus' feet; and he healed them. The people were amazed as they saw the dumb speaking, the crippled made whole, the lame walking, and the blind seeing; and they praised the God of Israel.

Some people brought him a man who was deaf and could hardly speak, and they begged Jesus to place his hand on him. So Jesus took him off alone, away from the crowd, put his fingers in the man's ears, spat, and touched the man's tongue. Then Jesus looked up to heaven, gave a deep groan, and said to the man, "Ephphatha," which means, "Open up!"

At once the man was able to hear, his speech impediment was removed, and he began to talk without any trouble. Then Jesus ordered the people not to speak of it to anyone; but the more he ordered them not to, the more they told it. And all who heard were completely amazed. "How well he does everything!" they exclaimed. "He even causes the deaf to hear and the dumb to speak!"

122 Jesus Feeds Four Thousand

Matthew 15:32-39; Mark 8:1-10

Not long afterward, another large crowd came together. When the people had nothing left to eat, Jesus called the disciples to him and said, "I feel sorry for these people, because they have been with me for three days and now have nothing to eat. If I send them home without feeding them, they will faint as they go, because some of them have come a long way."

His disciples asked him, "Where in this desert can anyone find enough food to feed all these people?"

"How much bread do you have?" Jesus asked.

"Seven loaves," they answered, "and a few small fish."

He ordered the crowd to sit down on the ground. Then he took the seven loaves and the fish, gave thanks to God, broke them, and gave them to his disciples, and the disciples gave them to the people. They all ate and had enough. Then the disciples took up seven baskets full of pieces left over.

The number of men who ate was four thousand, not counting the women and children.

Jesus sent the people away and at once got into a boat with his disciples and went to the district of Dalmanutha.

Insight: *Third journey - From Decapolis to Dalmanutha, Bethsaida and Caesarea Philippi.*

123 Demand for a Miracle

Matthew 15:32-39; Mark 8:1-10

Some Pharisees and Sadducees who came to Jesus wanted to trap him and started to argue with him. So they asked him to perform a miracle for them, to show that God approved of him. But Jesus answered, "When the sun is setting, you say, 'We are going to have fine weather, because the sky is red.' And early in the morning you say, 'It is going to rain, because the sky is red and dark.' When you see a cloud coming up in the west, at once you say that it is going to rain—and it does.

"And when you feel the south wind blowing, you say that it is going to get hot—and it does. Hypocrites! You can look at the earth and the sky and predict the weather; but you cannot interpret the signs concerning these times!

"Why, then, don't you know the meaning of this present time? How evil and godless are the people of this day!

"You ask me for a miracle? No! The only miracle you will be given is the miracle of Jonah."

Jesus gave a deep groan and said, "Why do the people of this day ask for a miracle? No, I tell you! No such proof will be given to these people!" He left them, got back into the boat, and started across to the other side of the lake.

124 Yeast of the Pharisees, Sadducees and Herod

Matthew 16:5-12; Mark 8:14-21

When the disciples crossed over to the other side of the lake, they had forgotten to bring enough bread and had only one loaf with them in the boat. "Take care," Jesus warned them, "and be on your guard against the yeast of the Pharisees and Sadducees and the yeast of Herod."

They started discussing among themselves: "He says this because we don't have any bread."

Jesus knew what they were saying, so he asked them, "Why are you discussing among yourselves about not having any bread? What little faith you have! Don't you know or understand yet? Are your minds so dull? You have eyes—can't you see? You have ears—can't you hear? Don't you remember when I broke the five loaves for the five thousand people? How many baskets full of leftover pieces did you take up?"

"Twelve," they answered.

"And when I broke the seven loaves for the four thousand people," asked Jesus, "how many baskets full of leftover pieces did you take up?"

"Seven," they answered.

"And you still don't understand?" he asked them. "How is it that you don't understand that I was not talking to you about bread? Guard yourselves from the yeast of the Pharisees and Sadducees!"

Then the disciples understood that he was not warning them to guard themselves from the yeast used in bread, but from the teaching of the Pharisees and Sadducees.

125 Jesus Heals a Blind Man at Bethsaida

Mark 8:22-26

They came to Bethsaida, where some people brought a blind man to Jesus and begged him to touch him. Jesus took the blind man by the hand and led him out of the village. After spitting on the man's eyes, Jesus placed his hands on him and asked him, "Can you see anything?"

The man looked up and said, "Yes, I can see people, but they look like trees walking around."

Jesus again placed his hands on the man's eyes. This time the man looked intently, his eyesight returned, and he saw everything clearly. Jesus then sent him home with the order, "Don't go back into the village."

126 Peter's Declaration about Jesus

Matthew16:13-20; Mark 8:27-30; Luke 9:18-20

Then Jesus and his disciples went away to the villages near Caesarea Philippi.

One day when Jesus was praying alone, the disciples came to him. He asked his disciples, "Who do men say the Son of Man is?"

"Some say John the Baptist," they answered. "Others say that you are Elijah, while others say Jeremiah or that one of the prophets of long ago has come back to life."

"What about you?" he asked them. "Who do you say I am?"

Simon Peter answered, "You are the Messiah, the Son of the living God."

"Good for you, Simon, son of John!" answered Jesus. "For this truth did not come to you from any human being, but it was given to you directly by my Father in heaven. And so I tell you, Peter: you are a rock, and on this rock foundation I will build my church, and not even death will ever be able to overcome it. I will give you the keys of the Kingdom of heaven; what you prohibit on earth will be prohibited in heaven, and what you permit on earth will be permitted in heaven."

Then Jesus ordered his disciples not to tell anyone that he was the Messiah.

127 Speaks about His Suffering and Death

Matthew 16:21-28; Mark 8:31-9:1; Luke 9:21-27

From that time on Jesus began to say plainly to his disciples, "I must go to Jerusalem. The Son of Man must suffer much and be rejected by the elders, the chief priests, and the teachers of the Law.

He will be put to death, but three days later he will rise to life."

He made this very clear to them. So Peter took him aside and began to rebuke him. "God forbid it, Lord!" he said. "That must never happen to you!" But Jesus turned around, looked at his disciples, and rebuked Peter.

"Get away from me, Satan! You are an obstacle in my way, because these thoughts of yours don't come from God, but from human nature."

Then Jesus said to his disciples, "If you want to come with me, you must forget yourself, take up your cross every day, and follow me. For if you want to save your own life, you will lose it; but if you lose your life for me and for the gospel, you will save it.

"Will you gain anything if you win the whole world but are yourself lost or defeated? Of course not! There is nothing you can give to regain your life. If you are ashamed of me and of my teaching in this godless and wicked day, then the Son of Man will be ashamed of you when he comes in his glory and in the glory of the Father and of the holy angels.

"For the Son of Man is about to come in the glory of his Father with his angels, and then he will reward each according to his deeds."

And he went on to say, "I tell you, there are some here who will not die until they have seen the Son of Man come as King—the Kingdom of God come with power." FP [He came to them after the resurrection as King, but he did not stay at this time.]

128 The Transfiguration

Mathew 17:1-13;Mark 9:2-13; Luke 9:28-36

Six days later Jesus took with him Peter and the brothers James and John and led them up a high mountain where they were alone. While he was praying, a change came over Jesus: his face changed its appearance and was shining like the sun, and his clothes became shining, dazzling white, whiter than anyone in the world could wash them.

Suddenly two men were there talking with him. They were Moses and Elijah, who appeared in heavenly glory and talked with Jesus about the way in which he would soon fulfill God's purpose by dying in Jerusalem. Peter and his companions were sound asleep, but they woke up and saw Jesus' glory and the two men who were standing with him.

As the men were leaving Jesus, Peter spoke up and said to Jesus, "Teacher, (Lord, Master), how good it is that we are here! If you wish, we will make three tents here, one for you, one for Moses, and one for Elijah." (He did not really know what he was saying.)

He and the others were so frightened that he did not know what to say.

While he was still speaking, a shining cloud appeared and covered them with its shadow; and the disciples were afraid as the cloud came over them. A voice said from the cloud, "This is my own dear Son, with whom I am well pleased, whom I have chosen—listen to him!"

When the disciples heard the voice, they were so terrified that they threw themselves face downward on the ground. Jesus came to them and touched them. "Get up," he said, "Don't be afraid!" So they looked up, took a quick look round and saw no one there but Jesus.

As they came down the mountain, Jesus ordered them, "Don't tell anyone about this vision you have seen until the Son of Man has been raised from death." The disciples kept quiet about all this and told no one at that time anything they had seen.

They obeyed this order, but among themselves they started discussing the matter, "What does this 'rising from death' mean? Then the disciples asked Jesus, "Why do the teachers of the Law say that Elijah has to come first?"

"Elijah is indeed coming first," answered Jesus, "and he will get everything ready. Yet why do the Scriptures say that the Son of Man will suffer much and be rejected? But I tell you that Elijah has already come and people did not recognize him, but treated him just as they pleased, as the Scriptures say about him. In the same way they will also mistreat the Son of Man."

Then the disciples understood that he was talking to them about John.

129 Jesus Heals Boy with Evil Spirit

Matthew 17:14-21; Mark 9:14-29; Luke 9:37-43a

The next day Jesus and the three disciples went down from the hill. When they joined the rest of the disciples, they saw a large crowd around them and some teachers of the Law arguing with them. When the people saw Jesus, they were greatly surprised, and ran to him and greeted him. Jesus asked his disciples, "What are you arguing with them about?"

A man in the crowd answered, "Teacher, I beg you, look at my son—my only son! He is an epileptic. A spirit attacks him with a sudden shout and throws him into a fit—such terrible attacks that he often falls in the fire or into water or to the ground, and he foams at the mouth, grits his teeth, and becomes stiff all over; it keeps on hurting him and will hardly let him go! I begged your disciples to drive the spirit out, but they could not."

Jesus answered, "How unbelieving and wrong you people are! How long must I stay with you? How long do I have to put up with you?"

Then he said to the man, "Bring your son here." They brought him to Jesus.

As soon as the spirit saw Jesus, the demon knocked him to the ground and threw him into a fit, so that he rolled around, foaming at the mouth. "How long has he been like this?" Jesus asked the father.

"Ever since he was a child," he replied. "Have pity on us and help us, if you possibly can!"

"Yes," said Jesus, "If you yourself can! Everything is possible for the person who has faith."

The father at once cried out, "I do have faith, but not enough. Help me have more!"

Jesus noticed that the crowd was closing in on them, so he gave a command to the evil spirit. "Deaf and dumb spirit," he said, "I order you to come out of the boy and never go into him again!"

The spirit screamed, threw the boy into a bad fit, and came out. The boy looked like a corpse, and everyone said, "He is dead!" But Jesus took the boy by the hand and helped him rise, and he stood up. He gave him back to his father. All the people were amazed at the mighty power of God.

After Jesus had gone indoors, his disciples came to Jesus in private and asked him, "Why couldn't we drive the demon out?"

"It was because you do not have enough faith," answered Jesus. "I assure you that if you have faith as big as a mustard seed, you can say to this hill, 'Go from here to there!' and it will go. You could do anything! Only prayer can drive this kind out," answered Jesus, "Nothing else can."

130 Jesus Speaks about His Death

Matthew 17:22-23; Mark 9:30-32; Luke 9:43b-45

The people were still marveling at everything Jesus was doing. Jesus and his disciples left that place and went on through Galilee. Jesus did not want anyone to know where he was, because he was teaching his disciples: "Don't forget what I am about to tell you! The Son of Man will be handed over to those who will kill him. Three days later, however, he will rise to life."

The disciples became very sad. They did not understand what this teaching meant. It had been hidden from them so that they could not understand it, and they were afraid to ask him about the matter.

Insight: Fourth *journey - From Caesarea Philippi to Capernaum.*

131 Payment of the Temple Tax

Matthew 17:24-27

When Jesus and his disciples came to Capernaum, the collectors of the Temple tax came to Peter and asked, "Does your teacher pay the Temple tax?"

"Of course," Peter answered.

When Peter went into the house, Jesus spoke up first, "Simon, what is your opinion? Who pays duties or taxes to the kings of this world? The citizens of the country or the foreigners?"

"The foreigners," answered Peter.

"Well, then," replied Jesus, "that means that the citizens don't have to pay. But we don't want to offend these people. So go to the lake and drop in a line. Pull up the first fish you hook, and in its mouth you will find a coin worth enough for my temple tax and yours. Take it and pay them our taxes."

132 Who is the Greatest?

Matthew 18:1-5; Mark 9:33-37; Luke 9:46-48

After going indoors Jesus asked his disciples, "What were you arguing about on the road?"

But they would not answer him, because on the road they had been arguing among themselves about who was the greatest.

Jesus sat down, called a child to come and stand in front of them by his side. He put his arms around him and said to them, "I assure you that unless you change and become like children, you will never enter the Kingdom of heaven. The greatest in the Kingdom of heaven is the one who humbles himself and becomes like this child. Whoever wants to be first must place himself last of all and be the servant of all.

"Whoever welcomes in my name one of these children, welcomes me; and whoever welcomes me, welcomes not only me but also the one who sent me. For the one who is least among you all is the greatest."

133 Who is Not Against You is for You

Mark 9:38-41; Luke 9:49-50

John said to him, "Teacher, we saw a man who was driving out demons in your name, and we told him to stop, because he doesn't belong to our group."

"Do not try to stop him," Jesus told them, "because no one who performs a miracle in my name will be able soon afterward to say evil things about me. For whoever is not against us is for us. I assure you that anyone who gives you a drink of water because you belong to me will certainly receive a reward."

134 Temptation to Sin

Matthew 18:6-11; Mark 9:42-48; Luke 17:1-3a

Jesus said to his disciples, "Things that make people fall into sin are bound to happen. If anyone should cause one of these little ones to lose his faith in me, it would be better for that person to have a large millstone tied around his neck and be drowned in the deep sea. How terrible for the world that there are things that make people lose their faith! Such things will always happen but how terrible for the one who causes them!

"So if your hand makes you lose your faith, cut it off! It is better for you to enter life without a hand than to keep both hands and go off to hell, to the fire that never goes out. And if your foot makes you lose your faith, cut it off! It is better for you to enter life without a foot than to keep both feet and be thrown into hell. And if your eye makes you lose your faith, take it out! It is better for you to enter the Kingdom of God with only one eye, than to keep both eyes and be thrown into hell. There 'the worms that eat them never die, and the fire that burns them is never put out.'

"See that you don't despise any of these little ones. Their angels in heaven, I tell you, are always in the presence of my Father in heaven."

135 Jesus and His Brothers

John 7:1-9

After this, Jesus traveled in Galilee; he did not want to travel in Judea, because the Jewish authorities there were wanting to kill him. The time for the Festival of Shelters was near, so Jesus' brothers said to him, "Leave this place and go to Judea, so that your followers will see the works that you are doing. People don't hide what they are doing if they want to be well known. Since you are doing these things, let the whole world know about you!" (Not even his brothers believed in him.)

Jesus said to them, "The right time for me has not yet come. Any time is right for you. The world cannot hate you, but it hates me, because I keep telling it that its ways are bad. You go on to the festival. I am not going to this festival, because the right time has not come for me." He said this and then stayed on in Galilee."

VI. PERIOD OF JUDEAN MINISTRY

The Judean Ministry, a period of about three months, covers the time from the Festival of Shelters to the Feast of Dedication and involves only two journeys:

From Capernaum to Jerusalem
From Jerusalem to Bethabara

Insight: *First journey - From Capernaum to Jerusalem*

136 A Samaritan Village Refuses to Receive Jesus

Luke 9:51-56; John 7:10

After his brothers had gone to the festival, Jesus also went. However, he did not go openly, but secretly. He made up his mind and set out on his way to Jerusalem. He sent messengers ahead of him, who went into a village in Samaria to get everything ready for him. But the people there would not receive him, because it was clear that he was on his way to Jerusalem. When the disciples James and John saw this, they said, "Lord, do you want us to call fire down from heaven and destroy them?"

Jesus turned and rebuked them. Then Jesus and his disciples went on to another village.

137 Ten Lepers Cleansed

Luke 17:11-19

As Jesus made his way to Jerusalem, he went along the border between Samaria and Galilee. He was going into a village when he was met by ten men suffering from a dreaded skin disease. They stood at a distance and shouted, "Jesus! Master! Have pity on us!"

Jesus saw them and said to them, "Go and let the priests examine you."

On the way they were made clean. When one of them saw that he was healed, he came back, praising God in a loud voice. He threw himself to the ground at Jesus' feet and thanked him. The man was a Samaritan. Jesus spoke up, "There were ten men who were healed; where are the other nine? Why is this foreigner the only one who came back to give thanks to God?"

And Jesus said to him, "Get up and go; your faith has made you well."

138 The Good Samaritan
Luke 10:25-37

A teacher of the Law came up and tried to trap Jesus. "Teacher," he asked, "what must I do to receive eternal life?"

Jesus answered him, "What do the Scriptures say? How do you interpret them?"

The man answered, " 'Love the Lord your God with all your heart, with all your soul, with all your strength, and with all your mind'; and, 'Love your neighbor as you love yourself.' "

"You are right," Jesus replied; "do this and you will live."

But the teacher of the Law wanted to justify himself, so he asked Jesus, "Who is my neighbor?"

Jesus answered, "There was once a man who was going down from Jerusalem to Jericho when robbers attacked him, stripped him, and beat him up, leaving him half dead.

"It so happened that a priest was going down that road; but when he saw the man, he walked on by on the other side.

"In the same way a Levite also came there, went over and looked at the man, and then walked on by on the other side.

"But a Samaritan who was traveling that way came upon the man, and when he saw him, his heart was filled with pity. He went over to him, poured oil and wine on his wounds and bandaged them; then he put the man on his own animal and took him to an inn, where he took care of him. The next day he took out two silver coins and gave them to the innkeeper. 'Take care of him,' he told the innkeeper, 'and when I come back this way, I will pay you back whatever else you spend on him.' "

And Jesus concluded, "In your opinion, which one of these three acted like a neighbor towards the man attacked by the robbers?"

The teacher of the Law answered, "The one who was kind to him."

Jesus replied, "You go, then, and do the same."

139 Jesus Visits Martha and Mary
Luke 10:38-42

As Jesus and his disciples went on their way, he came to a village where a woman named Martha welcomed him in her home. She had a sister named Mary, who sat down at the feet of the Lord and listened to his teaching. Martha was upset over all the work she had to do, so she came and said, "Lord, don't you care that my sister has left me to do all the work by myself? Tell her to come and help me!"

The Lord answered her, "Martha, Martha! You are worried and troubled over so many things, but just one is needed. Mary has chosen the right thing, and it will not be taken away from her."

140 Jesus at the Festival of Shelters

John 7:11-24

The Jewish authorities were looking for Jesus at the festival. "Where is he?" they asked.

There was much whispering about him in the crowd. "He is a good man," some people said. "No," others said, "he fools the people." But no one talked about him openly, because they were afraid of the Jewish authorities.

The festival was nearly half over when Jesus went to the Temple and began teaching. The Jewish authorities were greatly surprised and said, "How does this man know so much when he has never been to school?"

Jesus answered, "What I teach is not my own teaching, but comes from God, who sent me. Whoever is willing to do what God wants will know whether what I teach comes from God or whether I speak on my own authority. Those who speak on their own authority are trying to gain glory for themselves. But he who wants glory for the one who sent him is honest, and there is nothing false in him.

"Moses gave you the Law, didn't he? But not one of you obeys the Law. Why are you trying to kill me?"

"You have a demon in you!" the crowd answered. "Who is trying to kill you?"

Jesus answered, "I performed one miracle, and you were all surprised.

"Moses ordered you to circumcise your sons (although it was not Moses but your ancestors who started it), and so you circumcise a boy on the Sabbath. If a boy is circumcised on the Sabbath so that Moses' Law is not broken, why are you angry with me because I made a man completely well on the Sabbath?

"Stop judging by external standards, and judge by true standards."

141 Is He the Messiah?

John 7:25-31

Some of the people of Jerusalem said, "Isn't this the man the authorities are trying to kill? Look! He is talking in public, and they say nothing against him! Can it be that they really know that he is the Messiah? But when the Messiah comes, no one will know where he is from. And we all know where this man comes from."

Then they tried to seize him, but no one laid a hand on him, because his hour had not yet come. But many in the crowd believed in him and said, "When the Messiah comes, will he perform more miracles than this man has?"

142 Guards Sent to Arrest Jesus

John 7:32-36

The Pharisees heard the crowd whispering these things about Jesus, so they and the chief priests sent some guards to arrest him.

Jesus said, "I shall be with you a little while longer, and then I shall go away to him who sent me. You will look for me, but you will not find me, because you cannot go where I will be."

The Jewish authorities said among themselves, "Where is he about to go so that we shall not find him? Will he go to the Greek cities where our people live, and teach the Greeks? He says that we will look for him but will not find him, and that we cannot go where he will be. What does he mean?"

143 Streams of Life-giving Water

John 7:37-39

On the last and most important day of the festival Jesus stood up and said in a loud voice, "Whoever is thirsty should come to me and drink. As the scripture says, 'Streams of life-giving water will pour out from his side.'" FP [At his crucifixion, when his side was pierced, both blood and water poured forth. Both are life-giving to believers.]

Jesus said this about the Spirit, which those who believed in him were going to receive. At that time the Spirit had not yet been given, because Jesus had not been raised to glory.

144 Division among the People

John 7:40-44

Some of the people in the crowd heard him say this and said, "This man is really the Prophet!"

Others said, "He is the Messiah!"

But others said, "The Messiah will not come from Galilee! The scripture says that the Messiah will be a descendant of King David and will be born in Bethlehem, the town where David lived." So there was a division in the crowd because of Jesus. Some wanted to seize him, but no one laid a hand on him.

145 Unbelief of the Jews

John 7:45-52

When the guards went back, the chief priests and Pharisees asked them, "Why did you not bring him?"

The guards answered, "Nobody has ever talked the way this man does!"

"Did he fool you, too?" the Pharisees asked them. "Have you ever known one of the authorities or one Pharisee to believe in Him? This crowd does not know the Law of Moses, so they are under God's curse!"

One of the Pharisees there was Nicodemus, the man who had gone to see Jesus before.

He said to the others, "According to our Law we cannot condemn people before hearing them and finding out what they have done."

"Well," they answered, "are you also from Galilee? Study the Scriptures and you will learn that no prophet ever comes from Galilee."

146 Woman Caught in Adultery

John 8:1-11

Then everyone went home, but Jesus went to the Mount of Olives. Early the next morning he went back to the Temple.

All the people gathered around him, and he sat down and began to teach them. The teachers of the Law and the Pharisees brought in a woman who had been caught committing adultery, and they made her stand before them all.

"Teacher," they said to Jesus, "this woman was caught in the very act of committing adultery. In our Law Moses commanded that such a woman must be stoned to death. Now, what do you say?"

They said this to trap Jesus, so they could accuse him. But he bent over and wrote on the ground with his finger. As they stood there asking him questions, he straightened up and said to them, "Whichever one of you has committed no sin may throw the first stone at her." Then he bent over again and wrote on the ground.

When they heard this, they all left, one by one, the older ones first. Jesus was left alone, with the woman still standing there.

He straightened up and said to her, "Where are they? Is there no one left to condemn you?"

"No one, sir," she answered.

"Well, then," Jesus said, "I do not condemn you either. Go, but do not sin again."

147 Jesus the Light of the World

John 8:12-20

Jesus spoke to the Pharisees again. "I am the light of the world," he said. "Whoever follows me will have the light of life and will never walk in the darkness."

The Pharisees said to him, "Now you are testifying on your own behalf; what you say proves nothing."

"No," Jesus answered, "even though I do testify on my own behalf, what I say is true, because I know where I came from and where I am going. You do not know where I came from or where I am going. You make judgments in a purely human way; I pass judgment on no one.

But if I were to do so, my judgment would be true, because I am not alone in this; the Father who sent me is with me.

"It is written in your Law that when two witnesses agree, what they say is true. I testify on my own behalf, and the Father who sent me also testifies on my behalf."

"Where is your father?" they asked him.

"You know neither me nor my Father," Jesus answered. "If you knew me, you would know my Father also."

Jesus said all this as he taught in the Temple, in the room where the offering boxes were placed. And no one arrested him, because his hour had not come.

148 You Cannot Go Where I am Going

John 8:21-30

Again Jesus said to them, "I will go away; you will look for me, but you will die in your sins. You cannot go where I am going."

So the Jewish authorities said, "He says that we cannot go where he is going. Does this mean that he will kill himself?"

Jesus answered, "You belong to this world here below, but I come from above. You come from this world, but I am not from this world. That is why I told you that you will die in your sins. And you will die in your sins if you do not believe that 'I Am Who I Am.'"

"Who are you?" they asked him.

Jesus answered, "What I have told you from the very beginning. I have much to say about you, much to condemn you for. The one who sent me, however, is truthful, and I tell the world only what I have heard from him."

They did not understand that Jesus was talking to them about the Father. So he said to them, "When you lift up the Son of Man, you will know that 'I Am Who I Am'; then you will know that I do nothing on my own authority, but I say only what the Father has instructed me to say. And he who sent me is with me; he has not left me alone, because I always do what pleases him."

Many who heard Jesus say these things believed in him.

149 Free Men and Slaves

John 8:31-47

So Jesus said to those who believed in him, "If you obey my teaching, you are really my disciples; you will know the truth, and the truth will set you free."

"We are the descendants of Abraham," they answered, "and we have never been anybody's slaves. What do you mean, then, by saying, 'You will be free?"

Jesus said to them, "I am telling you the truth: everyone who sins is a slave of sin.

"A slave does not belong to a family permanently, but a son belongs there forever. If the Son sets you free, then you will be really free. I know you are Abraham's descendants.

"Yet you are trying to kill me, because you will not accept my teaching.

"I talk about what my Father has shown me, but you do what your father has told you."

They answered him, "Our father is Abraham."

"If you really were Abraham's children," Jesus replied, "you would do the same things that he did. All I have ever done is to tell you the truth I heard from God, yet you are trying to kill me. Abraham did nothing like this! You are doing what your father did."

"God himself is the only Father we have," they answered, "and we are his true children."

Jesus said to them, "If God really were your Father, you would love me, because I came from God and now I am here. I did not come on my own authority, but he sent me. Why do you not understand what I say? It is because you cannot bear to listen to my message.

"You are the children of your father, the Devil, and you want to follow your father's desires. From the very beginning he was a murderer and has never been on the side of truth, because there is no truth in him. When he tells a lie, he is only doing what is natural to him, because he is a liar and the father of all lies. But I tell the truth, and that is why you do not believe me.

"Which one of you can prove that I am guilty of sin? If I tell the truth, then why do you not believe me? He who comes from God listens to God's words. You, however, are not from God, and that is why you will not listen."

150 Jesus and Abraham

John 8:48-59

They asked Jesus, "Were we not right in saying that you are a Samaritan and have a demon in you?"

"I have no demon," Jesus answered. "I honor my Father, but you dishonor me. I am not seeking honor for myself. But there is one who is seeking it and who judges in my favor. I am telling you the truth: whoever obeys my teaching will never die."

They said to him, "Now we know for sure that you have a demon! Abraham died, and the prophets died, yet you say that whoever obeys your teaching will never die. Our father Abraham died; you do not claim to be greater than Abraham, do you? And the prophets also died. Who do you think you are?"

Jesus answered, "If I were to honor myself, that honor would be worth nothing.

The one who honors me is my Father - the very one you say is your God. You have never known him, but I know him.

"If I were to say that I do not know him, I would be a liar like you. But I do know him, and I obey his word. Your father Abraham rejoiced that he was to see the time of my coming; he saw it and was glad."

They said to him, "You are not even fifty years old and you have seen Abraham?"

"I am telling you the truth," Jesus replied. "Before Abraham was born, 'I Am'."

Then they picked up stones to throw at him, but Jesus hid himself and left the Temple.

151 Jesus Heals a Man Born Blind

John 9:1-12

As Jesus was walking along, he saw a man who had been born blind. His disciples asked him, "Teacher, whose sin caused him to be born blind? Was it his own or his parents' sins?"

Jesus answered, "His blindness has nothing to do with his sins or his parents' sins. He is blind so that God's power might be seen at work in him. As long as it is day, we must do the work of him who sent me; night is coming when no man can work. While I am in the world, I am the light for the world."

After he said this, Jesus spat on the ground and made some mud with the spittle; he rubbed the mud on the man's eyes and told him, "Go and wash your face in the Pool of Siloam." (This name means "Sent.") So the man went, washed his face, and came back seeing.

His neighbors, then, and the people who had seen him begging before this, asked, "Isn't this the man who used to sit and beg?"

Some said, "He is the one," but others said, "No he isn't; he just looks like him."

So the man himself said, "I am the man."

"How is it that you can now see?" they asked him.

He answered, "The man called Jesus made some mud, rubbed it on my eyes, and told me to go to Siloam and wash my face. So I went, and as soon as I washed, I could see."

"Where is he?" they asked.

"I don't know," he answered.

152 Pharisees Investigate the Healing

John 9:13-34

Then they took to the Pharisees the man who had been blind. The day that Jesus made the mud and cured him of his blindness was a Sabbath. The Pharisees, then, asked the man again how he had received his sight. He told them, "He put some mud on my eyes; I washed my face, and now I can see."

Some of the Pharisees said, "The man who did this cannot be from God, for he does not obey the Sabbath law."

Others, however said, How could a man who is a sinner perform such miracles as these?" And there was a division among them.

So the Pharisees asked the man once more, "You say he cured you of your blindness? Well, what do you say about him?"

"He is a prophet," the man answered.

The Jewish authorities, however, were not willing to believe that he had been blind and could now see, until they called his parents and asked them, "Is this your son? You say that he was born blind; how is it, then, that he can now see?"

His parents answered, "We know that he is our son, and we know that he was born blind. But we do not know how it is that he is now able to see, nor do we know who cured him of his blindness. Ask him; he is old enough, and he can answer for himself!"

His parents said this because they were afraid of the Jewish authorities, who had already agreed that anyone who said he believed that Jesus was the Messiah would be expelled from the synagogue. That is why his parents said, "He is old enough; ask him!"

A second time they called back the man who had been born blind, and said to him, "Promise before God that you will tell the truth! We know that this man who cured you is a sinner."

"I do not know if he is a sinner or not," the man replied. "One thing I do know: I was blind, and now I see."

"What did he do to you?" they asked. "How did he cure you of your blindness?"

"I have already told you," he answered, "and you would not listen. Why do you want to hear it again? Maybe you, too, would like to be his disciples?"

They insulted him and said, "You are that fellow's disciple; but we are Moses' disciples. We know that God spoke to Moses; as for that fellow, however, we do not even know where he comes from!"

The man answered, "What a strange thing that is! You do not know where he comes from, but he cured me of my blindness! We know that God does not listen to sinners; he does listen to people who respect him and do what he wants them to do. Since the beginning of the world nobody has ever heard of anyone giving sight to a person born blind. Unless this man came from God, he would not be able to do a thing."

They answered, "You were born and brought up in sin and you are trying to teach us?" And they expelled him from the synagogue.

153 Spiritual Blindness

John 9:33-41

When Jesus heard what had happened, he found the man and asked him, "Do you believe in the Son of Man?"

The man answered, "Tell me who he is, sir, so that I can believe in him!"

Jesus said to him, "You have already seen him, and he is the one who is talking with you now."

"I believe, Lord!" the man said, and knelt down before Jesus.

Jesus said, "I came to this world to judge, so that the blind should see and those who see should become blind."

Some Pharisees who were there with him heard him say this and asked him, "Surely you don't mean that we are blind, too?"

Jesus answered, "If you were blind, then you would not be guilty; but since you claim that you can see, this means that you are still guilty."

154 Parable of the Shepherd

John 10:1-6

Jesus said, "I am telling you the truth: the man who does not enter the sheep pen by the gate, but climbs in some other way, is a thief and a robber. The man who goes in through the gate is the shepherd of the sheep. The gatekeeper opens the gate for him; the sheep hear his voice as he calls his own sheep by name, and he leads them out. When he has brought them out, he goes ahead of them, and the sheep follow him, because they know his voice. They will not follow someone else; instead, they will run away from such a person, because they do not know his voice."

Jesus told them this parable, but they did not understand what he meant.

155 Jesus and the Good Shepherd

John 7:10-21

So Jesus said again, "I am telling you the truth: I am the gate for the sheep. All others who came before me are thieves and robbers, but the sheep did not listen to them. I am the gate. Those who come in by me will be saved; they will come in and go out and find pasture. The thief comes only in order to steal, kill, and destroy. I have come in order that you might have life - life in all its fullness.

"I am the good shepherd, who is willing to die for the sheep. When the hired man, who is not a shepherd and does not own the sheep, sees a wolf coming, he leaves the sheep and runs away; so the wolf snatches the sheep and scatters them. The hired man runs away because he is only a hired man and does not care about the sheep. I am the good shepherd.

"As the Father knows me and I know the Father, in the same way I know my sheep and they know me. And I am willing to die for them. There are other sheep which belong to me that are not in this sheep pen. I must bring them, too; they will listen to my voice, and they will become one flock with one shepherd.

"The Father loves me because I am willing to give up my life, in order that I may receive it back again. No one takes my life away from me. I give it up of my own free will. I have the right to give it up, and I have the right to take it back. That is what my Father has commanded me to do."

Again there was a division among the people because of these words. Many of them were saying, "He has a demon! He is crazy! Why do you listen to him?"

But others were saying, "A man with a demon could not talk like this! How could a demon give sight to blind people?"

Insight: *Second Journey - From Jerusalem to Bethabara.*

156 Jesus Rejected by the Jews

John 10:22-42

It was winter, and the Festival of the Dedication of the Temple was being celebrated in Jerusalem. Jesus was walking in Solomon's Porch in the Temple, when the people gathered around him and asked, "How long are you going to keep us in suspense? Tell us the plain truth: are you the Messiah?"

Jesus answered, "I have already told you, but you would not believe me. The deeds I do by my Father's authority speak on my behalf; but you will not believe, for you are not my sheep. My sheep listen to my voice; I know them, and they follow me. I give them eternal life, and they shall never die. No one can snatch them away from me. What my Father has given me is greater than everything, and no one can snatch them away from the Father's care. The Father and I are one."

Then the people again picked up stones to throw at him. Jesus said to them, "I have done many good deeds in your presence which the Father gave me to do; for which one of these do you want to stone me?"

They answered, "We do not want to stone you because of any good deeds, but because of your blasphemy! You are only a man, but you are trying to make yourself God!"

Jesus answered, "It is written in your own Law that God said, 'You are gods.' We know that what the scripture says is true forever; and God called those people gods, the people to whom his message was given. As for me, the Father chose me and sent me into the world.

"How, then, can you say that I blaspheme because I said that I am the Son of God? Do not believe me, then, if I am not doing the things my Father wants me to do. But if I do them, even though you do not believe me, you should at least believe my deeds, in order that you may know once and for all that the Father is in me and that I am in the Father."

Once more they tried to seize Jesus, but he slipped out of their hands.

Jesus then went back again across the Jordan River to the place where John had been baptizing, and he stayed there. Many people came to him. "John performed no miracles," they said, "but everything he said about this man was true." And many people there believed in him.

VII. THE PERAEAN MINISTRY

The Peraean Ministry, a period of about four months, covers the events succeeding the Feast of Dedication to the anointing at Bethany, six days before the crucifixion and involves four journeys:
From Bethabara to Bethany
From Bethany to Ephraim, where he secluded himself from the rulers for several weeks (possibly instructing the twelve)
From Ephraim through Peraea to Jericho From Jericho to Bethany

Insight: *The Peraean Ministry, a period of about four months, covers the events succeeding the Feast of Dedication to the anointing at Bethany, six days before the crucifixion, and involves four journeys.*

Insight: *First journey - From Bethabara to Bethany.*

157 Death of Lazarus

John 11:1-16

A man named Lazarus, who lived in Bethany, became sick. Bethany was the town where Mary and her sister Martha lived. (This Mary was the one who poured the perfume on the Lord's feet and wiped them with her hair; it was her brother Lazarus who was sick.) The sisters sent Jesus a message, "Lord, your dear friend is sick."

When Jesus heard it, he said, "The final result of this sickness will not be the death of Lazarus; this has happened in order to bring glory to God, and it will be the means by which the Son of God will receive glory."

Jesus loved Martha and her sister and Lazarus. Yet when he received the news that Lazarus was sick, he stayed where he was for two more days. Then he said to the disciples, "Let us go back to Judea."

"Teacher," the disciples answered, "just a short time ago the people there wanted to stone you; and are you planning to go back?"

Jesus said, "A day has twelve hours, doesn't it? So those who walk in broad daylight do not stumble, for they see the light of this world. But if they walk during the night they stumble, because they have no light."

Jesus said this and then added, "Our friend Lazarus has fallen asleep, but I will go and wake him up."

The disciples answered, "If he is asleep, Lord, he will get well."

Jesus meant that Lazarus had died, but they thought he meant natural sleep.

So Jesus told them plainly, "Lazarus is dead, but for your sake I am glad that I was not with him, so that you will believe. Let us go to him."

Thomas (called the Twin) said to his fellow disciples, "Let us go along with the Teacher, so that we may die with him!"

158 Resurrection and the Life

John 11:17-27

When Jesus arrived, he found that Lazarus had been buried four days before. Bethany was less than two miles from Jerusalem, and many Judeans had come to see Martha and Mary to comfort them about their brother's death.

When Martha heard that Jesus was coming, she went out to meet him, but Mary stayed in the house. Martha said to Jesus, "If you had been here, Lord, my brother would not have died! But I know that even now God will give you whatever you ask him for."

"Your brother will rise to life," Jesus told her.

"I know," she replied, "that he will rise to life on the last day."

Jesus said to her, "I am the resurrection and the life. Those who believe in me will live, even though they die; and those who live and believe in me will never die. Do you believe this?"

"Yes, Lord!" she answered. "I do believe that you are the Messiah, the Son of God, who was to come into the world."

159 Jesus Weeps

John 11:28-37

"After Martha said this, she went back and called her sister Mary privately. "The Teacher is here," she told her, "and is asking for you."

When Mary heard this, she got up and hurried out to meet him. (Jesus had not yet arrived in the village, but was still in the place where Martha had met him.) The people who were in the house with Mary comforting her followed her when they saw her get up and hurry out. They thought that she was going to the grave to weep there.

Mary arrived where Jesus was, and as soon as she saw him, she fell at his feet. "Lord," She said, "If you had been here, my brother would not have died!"

Jesus saw her weeping, and he saw how the people with her were weeping also; his heart was touched, and he was deeply moved. "Where have you buried him?" he asked them.

"Come and see, Lord," they answered.

Jesus wept. "See how much he loved him!" the people said.

But some of them said, "He gave sight to the blind man, didn't he? Could he not have kept Lazarus from dying?"

160 Lazarus Brought to Life

John 11:38-44

Deeply moved once more, Jesus went to the tomb, which was a cave with a stone placed at the entrance.

"Take the stone away!" Jesus ordered.

Martha, the dead man's sister, answered, "There will be a bad smell, Lord. He has been buried four days!"

Jesus said to her, "Didn't I tell you that you would see God's glory if you believed?"

They took the stone away. Jesus looked up and said, "I thank you, Father, that you listen to me. I know that you always listen to me, but I say this for the sake of the people here, so that they will believe that you sent me." After he had said this, he called out in a loud voice, "Lazarus, come out!"

He came out, his hands and feet wrapped in grave cloths, and with a cloth around his face. "Untie him," Jesus told them, "and let him go."

161 Plot Against Jesus

John 11:45-57

Many of the people who had come to visit Mary saw what Jesus did, and they believed in him. But some of them returned to the Pharisees and told them what Jesus had done. So the Pharisees and the chief priests met with the Council and said, "What shall we do? Look at all the miracles this man is performing! If we let him go on in this way, everyone will believe in him, and the Roman authorities will take action and destroy our Temple and our nation!"

One of them, named Caiaphas, who was High Priest that year, said, "What fools you are! Don't you realize that it is better for you to have one man die for the people, instead of the whole nation destroyed?"

Actually, he did not say this of his own accord; rather, as he was High Priest that year, he was prophesying that Jesus was going to die for the Jewish people, and not only for them, but also to bring together into one body all the scattered people of God." FP

Insight: *Second journey - From Bethany to Ephraim, where Jesus secluded himself from the rulers for several weeks.*

From that day on the Jewish authorities made plans to kill Jesus. So Jesus did not travel openly in Judea, but left and went to a place near the desert, to a town named Ephraim, where he stayed with the disciples.

The time for the Passover Festival was near, and many people went up from the country to Jerusalem to perform the ritual of purification before the festival.

They were looking for Jesus, and as they gathered in the Temple, they asked one another, "What do you think? Surely he will not come to the festival, will he?"

The chief priests and the Pharisees had given orders that if anyone knew where Jesus was, he must report it, so that they could arrest him.

162 A Warning Against Hypocrisy

Matthew 23:13-36; Luke 11:37-12:3

As thousands of people crowded together, so that they were stepping on each other, Jesus said first to his disciples, "Be on guard against the yeast of the Pharisees. I mean their hypocrisy. Whatever is covered up will be uncovered, and every secret will be made known.

"So then, whatever you have said in the dark will be heard in broad daylight, and whatever you have whispered in private in a closed room will be shouted from the housetops."

When Jesus finished speaking, a Pharisee invited him to eat with him; so he went in and sat down to eat. The Pharisee was surprised when he noticed that Jesus had not washed before eating.

So the Lord said to him, "How terrible for you, teachers of the Law and Pharisees! You hypocrites! You clean the outside of your cup and plate, while the inside is full of what things you have gotten by violence and selfishness and evil. Blind Pharisees. Fools! Did not God, who made the outside, also make the inside? Clean what is inside the cup first, and then the outside will be clean too! But give what is in your cups and plates to the poor, and everything will be ritually clean for you.

"How terrible for you, Teachers of the Law and Pharisees!! You hypocrites! You give to God one tenth even of the seasoning herbs, such as mint, dill, cumin, rue and all the other herbs, but you neglect to obey the really important teachings of the Law, such as justice and mercy and honesty and love for God. These you should practice, without neglecting the others. Blind guides! You strain a fly out of your drink, but swallow a camel!

"How terrible for you, Pharisees! You love the reserved seats in the synagogues and to be greeted with respect in the marketplaces. How terrible for you! You are like unmarked graves which people walk on without knowing it. You hypocrites! You are like the whitewashed tombs, which look fine on the outside but are full of bones and decaying corpses on the inside. In the same way, on the outside you appear good to everybody but inside you are full of hypocrisy and sins."

One of the teachers of the Law said to him, "Teacher, when you say this, you insult us too!"

Jesus answered, "How terrible also for you teachers of the Law! You put onto people's backs loads which are hard to carry, but you yourselves will not stretch out a finger to help them carry those loads.

"How terrible for you, teachers of the Law and Pharisees! You hypocrites! You make fine tombs for the prophets - the very prophets your ancestors murdered - and decorate the monuments of those who lived good lives; and you claim that if you had lived during the time of your ancestors, you would not have done what they did and killed the prophets.

"So you actually admit that you are the descendants of those who murdered the prophets! Go on, then, and finish up what your ancestors started! You snakes and children of snakes! How do you expect to escape from being condemned to hell? And so I tell you that I will send you prophets and wise men and teachers; you will kill some of them, crucify others, and whip others in the synagogues and chase them from town to town.

"For this reason the Wisdom of God said, 'I will send them prophets and messengers; they will kill some of them and persecute others!' FP So the people of this time will be punished for the murder of all the prophets killed since the creation of the world, from the murder of innocent Abel to the murder of Zechariah son of Berechiah, whom you murdered between the Temple and the altar. I tell you indeed: the punishment for all these will fall on the people of this day!

"How terrible for you, teachers of the Law and Pharisees! You hypocrites! You have kept the key that opens the door to the house of knowledge. You lock the door to the Kingdom of heaven in people's faces, but you yourselves don't go in, nor do you allow in those who are trying to enter!

"How terrible for you, teachers of the Law and Pharisees! You hypocrites! You sail the seas and cross whole countries to win one convert; and when you succeed, you make him twice as deserving of going to hell as you yourselves are!

"How terrible for you, blind guides! You teach, 'If someone swears by the Temple, he isn't bound by his vow; but if he swears by the gold in the Temple, he is bound.' Blind fools! Which is more important, the gold or the Temple which makes the gold holy?

"You also teach, 'If someone swears by the altar, he isn't bound by his vow; but if he swears by the gift on the altar, he is bound.' How blind you are! Which is the more important, the gift or the altar which makes the gift holy? So then, when a person swears by the altar, he is swearing by it and by all the gifts on it; and when he swears by the Temple, he is swearing by it and by God, who lives there; and when someone swears by heaven, he is swearing by God's throne and by him who sits on it."

Insight: *Third journey - From Ephraim through Peraea to Jericho.*

When Jesus left that place, the teachers of the Law and the Pharisees began to criticize him bitterly and ask him questions about many things, trying to lay traps for him and catch him saying something wrong.

163 Parable of the Rich Fool

Luke 12:13-21

A man in the crowd said to Jesus, "Teacher, tell my brother to divide with me the property our father left us."

Jesus answered him, "Friend, who gave me the right to judge or to divide the property between you two?"

And he went on to say to them all, "Watch out and guard yourselves from every kind of greed; because your true life is not made up of the things you own, no matter how rich you may be."

Then Jesus told them this parable: "There was once a rich man who had land which bore good crops. He began to think to himself, 'I don't have a place to keep all my crops. What can I do? This is what I will do,' he told himself; 'I will tear down my barns and build bigger ones, where I will store the grain and all my other goods. Then I will say to myself, ?Lucky man! You have all the good things you need for many years. Take life easy, eat, drink, and enjoy yourself!? But God said to him, 'You fool! This very night you will have to give up your life; then who will get all these things you have kept for yourself?'"

And Jesus concluded, "This is how it is with those who pile up riches for themselves but are not rich in God's sight."

164 Watchful Servants

Luke 12:35-40

"Be ready for whatever comes, dressed for action and your lamps lit, like servants who are waiting for their master to come back from a wedding feast. When he comes and knocks, they will open the door for him at once. How happy are those servants whose master finds them awake and ready when he returns! I tell you, he will take off his coat, have them sit down, and will wait on them.

"How happy are they if he finds them ready, even if he should come as late as midnight or even later! And you can be sure that if the owner of the house knew the time when the thief would come, he would not let the thief break into his house. And you, too, must be ready, because the Son of Man will come at an hour when you are not expecting him."

165 Faithful or Unfaithful Servant

Matthew 24:45-51; Luke 12:41-48

Peter said, "Lord, does this parable to apply to us, or do you mean it for everyone?"

The Lord answered, "Who, then, is the faithful and wise servant? He is the one that his master will put in charge of the other servants, to run the household and give the other servants their share of the food at the proper time. How happy that servant is if his master finds him doing this when he comes home!

"Indeed, I tell you, the master will put that servant in charge of all his property. But if that servant says to himself that his master is taking a long time to come back and if he begins to beat the other servants, both the men and the women, and eats and drinks and gets drunk, then the master will come back one day when the servant does not expect him and at a time he does not know.

"The master will cut him to pieces, and make him share the fate of the disobedient, the hypocrites. There he will cry and gnash his teeth.

"The servant who knows what his master wants him to do, but does not get himself ready and do it, will be punished with a heavy whipping. But the servant who does not know what his master wants, and yet does something for which he deserves a whipping, will be punished with a light whipping. Much is required from the person to whom much is given; much more is required from the person to whom much more is given."

166 Turn from Your Sins or Die

Luke 13:1-5

At that time some people were there who told Jesus about the Galileans whom Pilate had killed while they were offering sacrifices to God.

Jesus answered them, "Because these Galileans were killed in that way, do you think it proves that they were worse sinners than all other Galileans? No indeed! And I tell you that if you do not turn from your sins, you will all die as they did. What about those eighteen people in Siloam who were killed when the tower fell on them? Do you suppose this proves that they were worse than all the other people living in Jerusalem? No indeed! And I tell you that if you do not turn from your sins, you will all die as they did."

167 The Unfruitful Fig Tree

Luke 13:6-9

Then Jesus told them this parable: "There was once a man who had a fig tree growing in his vineyard. He went looking for figs on it but found none. So he said to his gardener, 'Look, for three years I have been coming here looking for figs on this fig tree and I haven't found any. Cut it down! Why should it go on using up the soil?

But the gardener answered, 'Leave it alone, sir, just one more year; I will dig around it and put in some fertilizer.

Then if the tree bears figs next year, so much the better; if not, then you can have it cut down!"

168 Jesus Heals Crippled Woman on the Sabbath

Luke 13:10-17

One Sabbath Jesus was teaching in a synagogue. A woman there had an evil spirit in her that had kept her sick for eighteen years; she was bent over and could not straighten up at all.

When Jesus saw her, he called out to her, "Woman, you are free from your sickness!"

He placed his hands on her, and at once she straightened herself up and praised God.

The official of the synagogue was angry that Jesus had healed on the Sabbath, so he spoke up and said to the people,

"There are six days in which we should work; so come during those days and be healed, but not on the Sabbath!"

The Lord answered him, "You hypocrites! Any one of you would untie his ox or his donkey from the stall and take it out to give it water on the Sabbath. Now here is this descendant of Abraham whom Satan has kept in bonds for eighteen years; should she not be released on the Sabbath?"

His answer made his enemies ashamed of themselves, while the people rejoiced over all the wonderful things that he did.

169 Jesus Heals a Sick Man

Luke 14:1-6

One Sabbath Jesus went to eat a meal at the home of one of the leading Pharisees; and people were watching Jesus closely. A man whose legs and arms were swollen came to Jesus, and Jesus spoke up and asked the teachers of the Law and the Pharisees, "Does our Law allow healing on the Sabbath or not?"

But they would not say a thing. Jesus took the man, healed him, and sent him away. Then he said to them, "If any one of you had a child or an ox that happened to fall in a well on a Sabbath, would you not pull it out at once on the Sabbath itself?"

But they were not able to answer him about this.

170 Parable of the Guests

Luke 14:7-14

Jesus noticed how some of the guests were choosing the best places, so he told this parable to all of them: "When someone invites you to a wedding feast, do not sit down in the best place. It could happen that someone more important than you has been invited, and your host, who invited both of you, would have to come and say to you, 'Let him have this place.'

"Then you would be embarrassed and have to sit in the lowest place. Instead, when you are invited, go and sit in the lowest place, so that your host will come to you and say, 'Come on up, my friend, to a better place'

"This will bring you honor in the presence of all the other guests. For those who make themselves great will be humbled, and those who humble themselves will be made great."

Then Jesus said to his host, "When you give a lunch or a dinner, do not invite your friends or your brothers or your relatives or your rich neighbors for they will invite you back, and in this way you will be paid for what you did.

"When you give a feast, invite the poor, the crippled, the lame, and the blind; and you will be blessed, because they are not able to pay you back. God will repay you on the day the good people rise from death."

171 Parable of the Wedding Feast

Matthew 22:1-14; Luke 14:15-24

When one of the guests sitting at the table heard this, he said to Jesus, "How happy are those who will sit at the feast in the Kingdom of God!"

Jesus again used parables in talking to the people. "The Kingdom of heaven is like this. Once there was a king who prepared a wedding feast for his son. He sent his servants to tell the invited guests to come to the feast, but they did not want to come. So he sent other servants with this message for the guests, 'My feast is ready now; my steers and prize calves have been butchered, and everything is ready. Come to the wedding feast!'

"But the invited guests paid no attention and went about their business. They all began, one after another, to make excuses. The first one told the servant, 'I have bought a field and must go and look at it; please accept my apologies.' Another one said, 'I have bought five pairs of oxen and am on my way to try them out; please accept my apologies.' Another one said, 'I have just gotten married, and for that reason I cannot come.' One went to his farm, another to his store, while others grabbed the servants, beat them, and killed them.

"The king was very angry; so he sent his soldiers, who killed those murderers and burned down their city. Then he called his servants and said to them, 'My wedding feast is ready, but the people I invited did not deserve it. Now hurry out to the main streets and alleys of the town, and bring back the poor, the crippled, the blind and the lame; invite to the feast as many people as you find.'

"So the servants went out into the streets and gathered all the people they could find, good and bad alike. Soon the servant said, 'Your order has been carried out, sir, but there is room for more.'

"So the master said to the servant, 'Go out to the country roads and lanes, and make people come in, so that my house will be full. I tell you all that none of those who were invited will taste my dinner!' "

"And the wedding hall was filled with people.

"The king went in to look at the guests and saw a man who was not wearing wedding clothes.

'Friend, how did you get in here without wedding clothes?' the king asked him. But the man said nothing. Then the king told the servants, 'Tie him up hand and foot, and throw him outside in the dark. There he will cry and gnash his teeth.'"

And Jesus concluded, "Many are invited, but few are chosen."

172 Parable of the Lost Sheep

Matt. 18:13-14; Luke 15:1-7

One day when many tax collectors and other outcasts came to listen to Jesus, the Pharisees and the teachers of the Law started grumbling, "This man welcomes outcasts and even eats with them!" So Jesus told them this parable:

"What do you think a man does who has one hundred sheep and loses one of them? What does he do? He leaves the other ninety-nine sheep grazing on the hillside in the pasture and goes looking for the one that got lost until he finds it. When he finds it, I tell you, he feels far happier over this one sheep than over the ninety-nine that did not get lost. He is so happy that he puts it on his shoulders, and carries it back home.

"Then he calls his friends and neighbors together and says to them, 'I am so happy I found my lost sheep. Let us celebrate!' In the same way, I tell you, there will be more joy in heaven over one sinner who repents than over ninety-nine respectable people who do not need to repent. In just the same way your Father in heaven does not want any of these little ones to be lost."

173 Parable of The Lost Coin

Luke 15:8-10

"Or suppose a woman who has ten silver coins loses one of them? What does she do? She lights a lamp, sweeps her house, and looks carefully everywhere until she finds it. When she finds it, she calls her friends and neighbors together, and says to them, 'I am so happy I found the coin I lost. Let us celebrate!' In the same way, I tell you, the angels of God rejoice over one sinner who repents."

174 Parable of The Lost Son

Luke 15:11-32

Jesus went on to say, "There was once a man who had two sons. The younger one said to him, 'Father, give me my share of the property now.' So the man divided the property between his two sons. After a few days the younger son sold his part of the property and left home with the money.

"He went to a country far away, where he wasted his money in reckless living. He spent everything he had. Then a severe famine spread over that country, and he was left without a thing.

So he went to work for one of the citizens of that country who sent him out to his farm to take care of the pigs. He wished he could fill himself with the bean pods the pigs ate, but no one gave him anything to eat.

"At last he came to his senses and said, 'All my father's hired workers have more than they can eat, and here I am, about to starve! I will get up and go to my father and say, "Father, I have sinned against God and against you. I am no longer fit to be called your son; treat me as one of your hired workers."'

So he got up and started back to his father.

"He was still a long way from home when his father saw him; his heart was filled with pity, and he ran, threw his arms round his son, and kissed him. 'Father,' the son said, 'I have sinned against God and against you. I am no longer fit to be called your son.'

"But the father called to his servants. 'Hurry!' he said. 'Bring the best robe and put it on him. Put a ring on his finger and shoes on his feet.

"Then go and get the prize calf and kill it, and let us celebrate with a feast! For this son of mine was dead, but now he is alive; he was lost, but now he has been found.' And so the feasting began.

"In the meantime the older son was out in the field. On his way back, when he came close to the house, he heard the music and dancing. So he called one of the servants and asked him, 'What's going on?' 'Your brother has come back home,' the servant answered, 'and your father has killed the prize calf, because he got him back safe and sound.'

"The older brother was so angry that he would not go into the house; so his father came out and begged him to come in. But he spoke back to his father, 'Look, all these years I have worked for you like a slave, and I have never disobeyed your orders. What have you given me? Not even a goat for me to have a feast with my friends! But this son of yours wasted all your property on prostitutes, and when he comes back home, you kill the prize calf for him!'

" 'My son,' the father answered, 'you are always here with me, and everything I have is yours. But we had to celebrate and be happy, because your brother was dead, but now he is alive; he was lost, but now he has been found.'"

175 The Shrewd Manager

Luke 16:1-12

Jesus said to his disciples, "There was once a rich man who had a servant who managed his property. The rich man was told that the manager was wasting his master's money, so he called him in and said, 'What is this I hear about you? Turn in a complete account of your handling of my property, because you cannot be my manager any longer.'

"The servant said to himself, 'My master is going to dismiss me from my job. What shall I do? I am not strong enough to dig ditches, and I am ashamed to beg. Now I know what I will do! Then when my job is gone, I shall have friends who will welcome me in their homes.'

"So he called in all the people who were in debt to his master. He asked the first one, 'How much do you owe my master?' 'One hundred barrels of olive oil,' he answered. 'Here is your account,' the manager told him; 'sit down and write fifty.' He asked another one, 'And you, how much do you owe?' 'A thousand bushels of wheat,' he answered, 'Here is your account,' the manager told him; 'write eight hundred.'

"As a result the master of this dishonest manager praised him for doing such a shrewd thing; because the people of this world are much more shrewd in handling their affairs than the people who belong to the light."

And Jesus went on to say, "And so I tell you: make friends for yourselves with worldly wealth, so that when it gives out you will be welcomed in the eternal home.

"Whoever is faithful in small matters will be faithful in large ones; whoever is dishonest in small matters will be dishonest in large ones.

"If, then, you have not been faithful in handling worldly wealth, how can you be trusted with true wealth? And if you have not been faithful with what belongs to someone else, who will give you what belongs to you?"

176 Some Sayings of Jesus

Luke 16:14-17

When the Pharisees heard all this, they made fun of Jesus, because they loved money.

Jesus said to them, "You are the ones who make yourselves look right in other people's sight, but God knows your hearts. For the things that are considered of great value by man are worth nothing in God's sight.

"The Law of Moses and the writings of the prophets were in effect up to the time of John the Baptist; since then the Good News about the Kingdom of God is being told, and everyone forces their way in. But it is easier for heaven and earth to disappear than for the smallest detail of the Law to be done away with."

177 Rich Man and Lazarus

Luke 16:19-31

"There was once a rich man who dressed in the most expensive clothes and lived in great luxury every day. There was also a poor man, named Lazarus, covered with sores, who used to be brought to the rich man's door, hoping to eat the bits of food that fell from the rich man's table. Even the dogs would come and lick his sores.

"The poor man died and was carried by the angels to sit beside Abraham at the feast in heaven.

"The rich man died and was buried, and in Hades, where he was in great pain, he looked up and saw Abraham, far away, with Lazarus at his side.

"So he called out, 'Father Abraham! Take pity on me, and send Lazarus to dip his finger in some water and cool off my tongue, because I am in great pain in this fire!'

"But Abraham said, 'Remember, my son, that in your lifetime you were given all the good things, while Lazarus got all the bad things. But now he is enjoying himself here, while you are in pain. Besides all that, there is a deep pit lying between us, so that those who want to cross over from here to you cannot do so, nor can anyone cross over to us from where you are.'

"The rich man said, 'Then I beg you, father Abraham, send Lazarus to my father's house, where I have five brothers. Let him go and warn them so that they, at least, will not come to this place of pain.'

"Abraham said, 'Your brothers have Moses and the prophets to warn them; your brothers should listen to what they say.'

"The rich man answered, 'That is not enough, father Abraham! But if someone were to rise from death and go to them, then they would turn from their sins.'

"But Abraham said, 'If they will not listen to Moses and the prophets, they will not be convinced even if someone were to rise from death.'"

178 Faith

Luke 17:5-6

The apostles said to the Lord, "Make our faith greater."

The Lord answered, "If you had faith as big as a mustard seed, you could say to this mulberry tree, 'Pull yourself up by the roots and plant yourself in the sea!' and it would obey you."

179 A Servant's Duty

Luke 17:7-10

"Suppose one of you has a servant who is ploughing or looking after the sheep. When he comes in from the field, do you tell him to hurry along and eat his meal? Of course not! Instead, you say to him, 'Get my supper ready, then put on your apron and wait on me while I eat and drink; after that you may have your meal.' The servant does not deserve thanks for obeying orders, does he? It is the same with you; when you have done all you have been told to do, say, 'We are ordinary servants; we have only done our duty.'"

180 The Widow and the Judge

Luke 18:1-8

Then Jesus told his disciples a parable to teach them that they should always pray and never become discouraged.

"In a certain town there was a judge who neither feared God nor respected man. And there was a widow in that same town who kept coming to him and pleading for her rights, saying, 'Help me against my opponent!'

"For a long time the judge refused to act, but at last he said to himself, 'Even though I don't fear God or respect people, yet because of all the trouble this widow is giving me, I will see to it that she gets her rights. If I don't, she will keep on coming and finally wear me out!"

And the Lord continued, "Listen to what the corrupt judge said. Now, will God not judge in favor of his own people who cry to him day and night for help? Will he be slow to help them? I tell you, he will judge in their favor and do it quickly. But will the Son of Man find faith on the earth when he comes?"

181 Pharisee and Tax Collector

Luke 18:9-14

Jesus also told this parable to people who were sure of their own goodness and despised everybody else.

"Once there were two men went up to the Temple to pray: one was a Pharisee, the other a tax collector. The Pharisee stood apart by himself and prayed, 'I thank you, God, that I am not greedy, dishonest, or an adulterer, like everybody else. I thank you that I am not like that tax collector over there. I fast two days a week, and I give you one tenth of all my income.'

"But the tax collector stood at a distance and would not even raise his face to heaven, but beat his breast and said, 'God, have pity on me, a sinner!'

"I tell you," said Jesus, "this tax collector, and not the Pharisee, was in the right with God when he went home. For those who make themselves great will be humbled, and those who humble themselves will be made great."

182 A Brother Who Sins

Matthew 18:15-17

"If your brother sins against you, go to him and show him his fault. But do it privately, just between yourselves. If he listens to you, you have won your brother back. But if he will not listen to you, take one or two other persons with you, so that 'every accusation may be upheld by the testimony of two or more witnesses,' as the scripture says. And if he will not listen to them, then tell the whole thing to the church. Finally, if he will not listen to the church, treat him as though he were a pagan or a tax collector."

183 Prohibiting and Permitting

Matthew 18:18-20

"And so I tell all of you: what you prohibit on earth will be prohibited in heaven, and what you permit on earth will be permitted in heaven.

"And I tell you more: whenever two of you on earth agree about anything you pray for, it will be done for you by my Father in heaven. For where two or three come together in my name, I am there with them."

184 The Unforgiving Servant

Matthew 18:21-35; Luke 17:3b-4

Then Peter came to Jesus and asked, "Lord, if my brother keeps on sinning against me, how many times do I have to forgive him? Seven times?"

"No, not seven times," answered Jesus, "but seventy times seven. If your brother sins, rebuke him, and if he repents, forgive him. If he sins against you seven times in one day, and each time he comes to you saying, 'I repent,' you must forgive him because the Kingdom of heaven is like this:

"Once there was a king who decided to check on his servants' accounts. He had just begun to do so when one of them was brought in who owed him millions of dollars.

"The servant did not have enough money to pay his debt, so the king ordered him to be sold as a slave, with his wife and his children and all that he had, in order to pay the debt.

"The servant fell on his knees before the king. 'Be patient with me,' he begged, 'and I will pay you everything!' The king felt sorry for him, so he forgave him the debt and let him go.

"Then the man went out and met one of his fellow servants who owed him a few dollars. He grabbed him and started choking him. 'Pay back what you owe me!' he said.

"His fellow servant fell down and begged him, 'Be patient with me and I will pay you back!' But he refused; instead, he had him thrown into jail until he should pay the debt. When the other servants saw what had happened, they were very upset and went to the king and told him everything.

"So he called the servant in. 'You worthless slave!' he said. 'I forgave you the whole amount you owed me, just because you asked me to. You should have had mercy on your fellow servant, just as I had mercy on you.'

"The king was very angry, and he sent the servant to jail to be punished until he should pay back the whole amount."

And Jesus concluded, "That is how my Father in heaven will treat every one of you unless you forgive your brother from your heart."

185 Jesus Teaches about Divorce

Matthew 19:1-12; Mark 10:1-12

When Jesus finished saying these things, he left Galilee and went to the territory of Judea on the other side of the Jordan River. Large crowds followed him, and he healed them there. He taught them, as he always did.

Some Pharisees came to him and tried to trap him by asking, "Does our Law allow a man to divorce his wife for whatever reason he wishes?"

Jesus answered, "Haven't you read the scripture that says that in the beginning the Creator made people male and female? And God said, 'For this reason a man will leave his father and mother and unite with his wife, and the two will become one.' So they are no longer two, but one. No human being must separate, then, what God has joined together."

The Pharisees asked him, "Why, then, did Moses give the law for a man to hand his wife a divorce notice and send her away?" Jesus answered, "Moses gave you permission to divorce your wives because you are so hard to teach. But it was not like that at the time of creation. I tell you, then, that any man who divorces his wife for any cause other than her unfaithfulness, commits adultery if he marries some other woman. In the same way, the woman who divorces her husband and marries another man commits adultery."

When they went back into the house, the disciples asked Jesus about this matter. They said to him, "If this is how it is between a man and his wife, it is better not to marry."

Jesus answered, "This teaching does not apply to everyone, but only to those to whom God has given it. For there are different reasons why men cannot marry; some, because they were born that way; others, because men made them that way; and others do not marry for the sake of the Kingdom of heaven. Let him who can accept this teaching do so."

186 Jesus Blesses the Little Children

Matthew 19:13-15; Mark 10:13-16, Luke 18:15-17

Some people brought children and babies to Jesus for him to place his hands on them and pray for them, but the disciples saw them and scolded them for doing so.

When Jesus noticed this, he was angry and said to his disciples, "Let the children come to me, and do not stop them, because the Kingdom of God belongs to such as these. I assure you that whoever does not receive the Kingdom of God like a child will never enter it."

Then he took the children in his arms, placed his hands on each of them, and blessed them and then went away.

187 The Rich Young Man

Matthew 19:16-30; Mark 10:17-31; Luke 18:18-30

As Jesus was starting on his way again, a man ran up, knelt before him, and asked him, "Good Teacher, what good thing must I do to receive eternal life?"

"Why do you call me good?" Jesus asked him. "Why do you ask me concerning what is good? There is only One who is good. Keep the commandments if you want to enter life."

"What commandments?" he asked.

Jesus answered, "You know the commandments: 'Do not commit murder; do not commit adultery; do not steal; do not accuse anyone falsely; do not cheat; respect your father and mother; and love your neighbor as yourself."

"Teacher," the young man said, "ever since I was young I have obeyed all these commandments. What else do I need to do?"

Jesus looked straight at him with love and said, "There is still one more thing you need to do. If you want to be perfect, go and sell all you have and give the money to the poor, and you will have riches in heaven; then come and follow me."

When the man heard this, gloom spread over his face, and he went away sad, because he was very rich.

Jesus saw that he was sad and looked around at his disciples and said to them, "How hard it will be for rich people to enter the Kingdom of God!"

The disciples were shocked at these words, but Jesus went on to say, "My children, how hard it is to enter the Kingdom of God! It is much harder for a rich man to enter the Kingdom of God than for a camel to go through the eye of a needle."

At this the disciples were completely amazed, and asked one another, "Who, then, can be saved?"

Jesus looked straight at them and answered, "This is impossible for human beings but not for God; everything is possible for God."

Then Peter spoke up, "Look, we have left everything - our homes - and followed you. What will we have?"

Jesus said to them, "You can be sure that when the Son of Man sits on his glorious throne in the age to come, then you twelve followers of mine will also sit on thrones, to rule the twelve tribes of Israel.

"And everyone who has left houses or brothers or sisters or father or mother or children or fields for my sake and for the gospel and for the sake of the Kingdom of God will receive much more in this present age. They will receive a hundred times more houses, brothers, sisters, mothers, children, and fields - and persecutions as well; and in the age to come they will receive eternal life."

188 Workers in the Vineyard

Matthew 20:1-16

"The Kingdom of heaven is like this. Once there was a man who went out early in the morning to hire some men to work in his vineyard. He agreed to pay them the regular wage, a silver coin a day, and sent them to work in his vineyard.

"He went out again to the marketplace at nine o'clock and saw some men standing there doing nothing, so he told them, 'You also go and work in the vineyard, and I will pay you a fair wage.' So they went.

"Then at twelve o'clock and again at three o'clock he did the same thing.

"It was nearly five o'clock when he went to the marketplace and saw some other men still standing there.

"'Why are you wasting the whole day here doing nothing?' he asked them.

"'No one hired us,' they answered.

"'Well, then, you go and work in the vineyard,' he told them.

"When evening came, the owner told his foreman, Call the workers and pay them their wages, starting with those who were hired last and ending with those who were hired first.'

"The men who had begun to work at five o'clock were paid a silver coin each. So when the men who were the first to be hired came to be paid, they thought they would get more; but they too were given a silver coin each. They took their money and started grumbling against the employer.

"'These men who were hired last worked only one hour,' they said, 'while we put up with a whole day's work in the hot sun - yet you paid them the same as you paid us!'

"'Listen, friend,' the owner answered one of them. 'I have not cheated you. After all, you agreed to do a day's work for one silver coin. Now, take your pay and go home. I want to give this man who was hired last as much as I gave you. Don't I have the right to do as I wish with my own money? Or are you jealous because I am generous?' "

And Jesus concluded, "So those who are last will be first, and those who are first will be last."

189 Jesus Speaks of His Death

Matthew 20:17-19; Mark 10:32-34; Luke 18:31-34

Jesus and his disciples were now on the road going up to Jerusalem.

Jesus was going ahead of the disciples who were filled with alarm; the people who followed behind were afraid. Once again Jesus took the twelve disciples aside and spoke to them privately, as they walked along, of the things that were going to happen to him.

"Listen," he told them, "we are going up to Jerusalem where the Son of Man will be handed over to the chief priests and the teachers of the Law, where everything the prophets wrote about the Son of Man will come true. They will condemn him to death and then hand him over to the Gentiles, who will make fun of him, spit on him, whip him, and crucify him, but three days later he will rise to life."

But the disciples did not understand any of these things; the meaning of the words was hidden from them, and they did not know what Jesus was talking about.

190 Request of James and John and Their Mother

Matthew 20:20-28; Mark 10:35-45

Then the wife of Zebedee came to Jesus with her two sons, James and John, bowed before him, and asked him for a favor. "Teacher, there is something we want you to do for us."

"What do you want?" Jesus asked her.

She answered, "Promise me that these two sons of mine will sit at your right and your left when you are King," and James and John answered, "When you sit on your throne in your glorious Kingdom, we want you to let us sit with you, one at your right and one at your left."

"You don't know what you are asking for," Jesus answered the sons. "Can you drink the cup of suffering that I must drink? Can you be baptized in the way I must be baptized?"

"We can," they answered.

Jesus said to them, "You will indeed drink the cup I must drink and be baptized in the way I must be baptized. But I do not have the right to choose who will sit at my right and my left. It is God who will give these places to those for whom he has prepared them."

When the other ten disciples heard about it, they became angry with James and John. So Jesus called them all together to him and said, "You know that those who are considered rulers of the heathen have power over them, and the leaders have complete authority. This, however, is not the way it is among you.

"If one of you wants to be great, he must be the servant of the rest; and if one of you wants to be first, he must be the slave of all. For even the Son of Man did not come to be served; he came to serve and to give his life to redeem many people."

191 Blind Bartimaeus Healed

Mark 10:46-52; Luke 18:35-43

As Jesus was coming near Jericho with his disciples and a large crowd, a blind beggar named Bartimaeus the son of Timaeus was sitting by the road. When he heard the crowd passing by he asked, "What is this?"

"Jesus of Nazareth is passing by," they told him.

When he heard that it was Jesus of Nazareth, he began to shout, "Jesus! Son of David! Have mercy on me!"

Many of the people scolded him and told him to be quiet. But he shouted even more loudly, "Son of David! Have mercy on me!"

So Jesus stopped and ordered that the blind man be brought to him.

So they called the blind man. "Cheer up!" they said. "Get up, he is calling you."

So he threw off his cloak, jumped up, and came to Jesus. When he came near, Jesus asked him, "What do you want me to do for you?"

"Teacher," the blind man answered, "I want to see again."

Jesus said to him, "Then see! Go, your faith has made you well."

At once he was able to see, and he followed Jesus, giving thanks to God. When the crowd saw it, they all praised God.

192 Jesus and Zacchaeus

Luke 19:1-10

Jesus went on into Jericho and was passing through. There was a chief tax collector there, named Zacchaeus, who was rich. He was trying to see who Jesus was, but he was a little man and could not see Jesus because of the crowd.

So he ran ahead of the crowd and climbed a sycamore tree to see Jesus, who was going to pass that way. When Jesus came to that place, he looked up and said to Zacchaeus, "Hurry down, Zacchaeus, because I must stay in your house today."

Zacchaeus hurried down and welcomed him with great joy. All the people who saw it started grumbling, "This man has gone as a guest to the home of a sinner!"

Zacchaeus stood up and said to the Lord, "Listen, sir! I will give half my belongings to the poor, and if I have cheated anyone, I will pay back four times as much."

Jesus said to him, "Salvation has come to this house today, for this man, also, is a descendant of Abraham. The Son of Man came to seek and to save the lost."

193 Jesus Heals Two Blind Men

Matthew 20:29-34

As Jesus and his disciples were leaving Jericho a large crowd was following. Two blind men who were sitting by the road heard that Jesus was passing by, so they began to shout, "Son of David! Have mercy on us, sir!"

The crowd scolded them and told them to be quiet. But they shouted even more loudly, "Son of David! Have mercy on us, sir!"

Jesus stopped and called them. "What do you want me to do for you?" he asked them.

"Sir," they answered, "we want you to give us our sight!"

Jesus had pity on them and touched their eyes; at once they were able to see, and they followed him.

Insight: *Fourth journey - From Jericho to Bethany*

194 Jesus Anointed at Bethany

John 12:1-8

Six days before the Passover, Jesus went to Bethany, the home of Lazarus, the man Jesus had raised from death. They prepared a dinner for him there, which Martha helped serve; Lazarus was one of those who were sitting at the table with Jesus.

Then Mary took a whole pint of a very expensive perfume made of pure nard, poured it on Jesus' feet, and wiped them with her hair. The sweet smell of the perfume filled the whole house.

A disciple named Judas Iscariot was there. He was the one who was going to betray Jesus, and he asked, "Why wasn't this perfume sold for three hundred silver coins and the money given to the poor?"

Judas did not really care about the poor. He asked this because he carried the money bag and sometimes would steal from it.

Jesus replied, "Leave her alone! She has kept this perfume for the day of my burial. You will always have the poor with you, but you won't always have me."

195. Plot Against Lazarus

John 12:9-11

A large number of people heard that Jesus was in Bethany, so they went there, not only because of Jesus but also to see Lazarus, whom Jesus had raised from death.

So the chief priests made plans to kill Lazarus too, because on his account many Jews were rejecting them and believing in Jesus.

VIII. JESUS' FINAL WEEK

INSIGHT: *The final week, a period of only six days, covers events from Jesus' triumphal entry into Jerusalem to his death on the cross. Each day he traveled from Bethany to Jerusalem to teach and heal in the Temple.*

The Passion Week, a period of only five days, covers events from Jesus triumphal entry into Jerusalem to his death on the cross and involves nine short journeys:

1 From Bethany to the Temple and return

2 From Bethany to the Temple, when he drove out the merchants, and return

3 From Bethany to the Temple and Mount of Olives and return

4 From Bethany to the Supper in the Upper Room

5 From the supper to the Garden of Gethsemane on Mount of Olives

6 From Gethsemane to the house of Annas, then to the house of Caiaphas, the High Priest and the Council

7 From Caiaphas to Pilate

8 From Pilate to Herod and return

9 From Pilate to Calvary

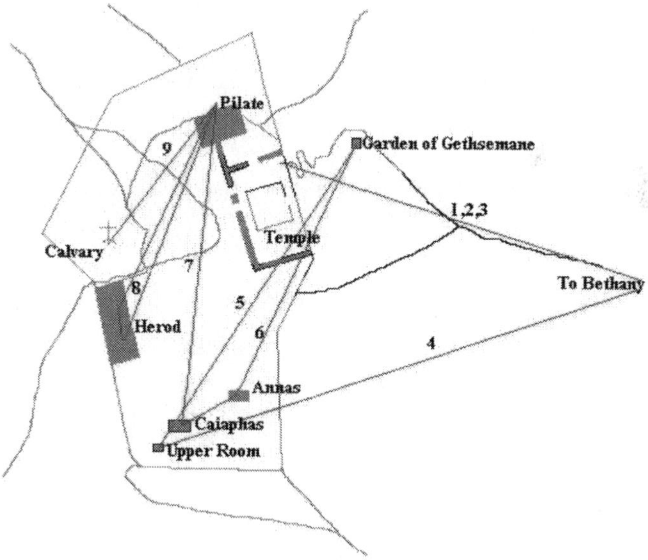

196 Jesus' Triumphant Entry into Jerusalem

Matthew 21:1-11; Mark 11:1-11; Luke 19:28-44; John 12:12-19

As Jesus and his disciples approached Jerusalem, they came near the towns of Bethphage and Bethany, at the Mount of Olives.

There Jesus sent two of the disciples on ahead with these instructions: "Go to the village there ahead of you, and at once you will find a donkey tied up with her colt beside her that has never been ridden. Untie them and bring them to me.

'If someone asks you why are you untying them, tell him, 'The Master needs them', and then he will let them go at once."

So the disciples went on their way and found a colt out in the street, tied to the door of a house, just as Jesus had told them. As they were untying the colt, its owners said to them, "Why are you untying it?"

They answered just as Jesus had told them, "The Master needs it," and the crowd let them go. They brought the donkey and the colt, threw their cloaks over them and helped Jesus get on.

The next day the large crowd that had come to the Passover Festival heard that Jesus was coming to Jerusalem. So they cut branches from the trees and spread them on the road. Many people spread their cloaks on the road. The people who were in front and those who followed behind began to shout, "Praise God! God bless him who comes in the name of the Lord! God bless the coming kingdom of David, our father! Praise be to God!"

When he came near Jerusalem, at the place where the road went down the Mount of Olives, the large crowd of his disciples began to thank God and praise him in loud voices for all the great things that they had seen: "God bless the king who comes in the name of the Lord! Peace in heaven, and glory to God!"

Then some of the Pharisees in the crowd spoke to Jesus. "Teacher," they said, "command your disciples to be quiet!"

Jesus answered, "I tell you that if they keep quiet, the stones themselves will start shouting."

This happened in order to make come true what the prophet had said:

"Tell the city of Zion, look, your king is coming to you!
He is humble and rides on a donkey, and on a colt,
the foal of a donkey."*FP Zechariah 9:9*

His disciples did not understand this at the time; but when Jesus had been raised to glory, they remembered that the scripture said this about him and that they had done this for him.

The people who had been with Jesus when he called Lazarus out of the grave and raised him from death had reported what had happened. That was why the crowd met him, because they heard that he had performed this miracle. The Pharisees then said to one another, "You see, we are not succeeding at all! Look, the whole world is following him!"

He came closer to the city, and when he saw it, he wept over it, saying, "If you only knew today what is needed for peace! But now you cannot see it! The time will come when your enemies will surround you with barricades, blockade you, and close in on you from every side. They will completely destroy you and the people within your walls; not a single stone will they leave in its place, because you did not recognize the time when God came to save you!"

When Jesus entered Jerusalem, the whole city was thrown in an uproar. "Who is he," the people asked.

"This is the prophet Jesus, from Nazareth in Galilee," the crowds answered.

197 Jesus Speaks about His Death

John 12:20-36

Some Greeks were among those who had gone to Jerusalem to worship during the festival. They came to Philip (he was from Bethsaida in Galilee) and said, "Sir, we want to see Jesus."

Philip went and told Andrew, and the two of them went and told Jesus.

Jesus answered them, "The hour has now come for the Son of Man to receive great glory. I am telling you the truth: a grain of wheat remains no more than a single grain unless it is dropped into the ground and dies. If it does die, then it produces many grains. Those who love their own life will lose it; those who hate their own life in this world will keep it for life eternal. Whoever wants to serve me must follow me, so that my servant will be with me where I am. And my Father will honor anyone who serves me.

"Now my heart is troubled and what shall I say? Shall I say, "Father, do not let this hour come upon me?" But that is why I came so that I might go through this hour of suffering. Father, bring glory to your name!"

Then a voice spoke from heaven, "I have brought glory to it, and I will do so again."

The crowd standing there heard the voice, and some of them said it was thunder, while others said, "An angel spoke to him!"

But Jesus said to them, "It was not for my sake that this voice spoke, but for yours. Now is the time for this world to be judged; now the ruler of this world will be overthrown. When I am lifted up from the earth, I will draw everyone to me." (In saying this he indicated the kind of death he was going to suffer.)

The crowd answered, "Our Law tells us that the Messiah will live forever. How, then, can you say that the Son of Man must be lifted up?

"Who is this Son of Man?"

Jesus answered, "The light will be among you a little longer. Continue on your way while you have the light, so the darkness will not come upon you; for the one who walks in the dark does not know where he is going.

"Believe in the light, then, while you have it, so that you will be the people of the light."

198 Unbelief of the Jews

Mark 11:11

After Jesus said this, he went off and hid himself from them. Even though he had performed all these miracles in their presence, they did not believe in him, so that what the prophet Isaiah had said might come true:

"Lord, who believed the message we told?
To whom did the Lord show his power?" FP Isaiah 53:1

And so they were not able to believe, because Isaiah also said:

"God has blinded their eyes, and closed their minds,
so that their eyes would not see,
and their minds would not understand,
and they would not turn to me, says God,
for me to heal them." FP Isaiah 6:10

Isaiah said this because he saw Jesus' glory and spoke about him.

Even then, many Jewish authorities believed in Jesus; but because of the Pharisees they did not talk about it openly, so as not to be expelled from the synagogue. They loved human approval rather than the approval of God.

Jesus said in a loud voice, "Whoever believes in me believes not only in me but also in him who sent me. Whoever sees me sees also him who sent me. I have come into the world as light, so that everyone who believes in me should not remain in the darkness.

"If people hear my message and do not obey it, I will not judge him. I came, not to judge the world, but to save it. Those who reject me and do not accept my message have one who will judge them. The words I have spoken will be their judge on the last day!

"This is true, because I have not spoken on my own authority, but the Father who sent me has commanded me what I must and speak. And I know that his command brings eternal life. What I say, then, is what the Father has told me to say."

Jesus went into the Temple, and looked around at everything. But since it was already late in the day, he went out to Bethany with the twelve disciples.

199 Jesus Curses the Fig Tree

Matthew 21:18-20a; Mark 11:12-14

On his way back to the city from Bethany, early next morning, Jesus was hungry. He saw in the distance a fig tree covered with leaves, so he went to see if he could find any figs on it. But when he came to it, he found only leaves, because it was not the right time for figs.

Jesus said to the fig tree, "You will never again bear fruit! No one shall ever eat figs from you again!"

And his disciples heard him.

200 Jesus Goes to the Temple

Matthew 21:12-17; Mark 11:15-19; Luke 19:45-48

When they arrived in Jerusalem, Jesus went to the Temple and began to drive out the merchants who were buying and selling there. He overturned the tables of the moneychangers and the stools of those who sold pigeons, and he would not let anyone carry anything through the Temple courtyards.

He then taught the people, "It is written in the Scriptures that God said, "My Temple will be called a house of prayer for all the people of all nations!" But you have turned it into a hideout for thieves!"

Every day Jesus taught in the temple. The blind and the crippled came to him in the Temple and he healed them. The chief priests and the teachers of the Law became angry when they saw the wonderful things he was doing and the children shouting in the Temple, "Praise to David's Son!" So they asked Jesus, "Do you hear what they are saying?"

"Indeed I do," answered Jesus. "Haven't you ever read this Scripture? "You have trained children and babies to offer perfect praise."

The chief priests, the teachers of the Law, and the leaders of the people heard of this and wanted to kill him, so they began looking for some way to kill Jesus. They were afraid of him, because the whole crowd was amazed at his teaching. All the people kept listening to him, not wanting to miss a single word.

When evening came, Jesus and his disciples went out of the city to Bethany, where he spent the night.

201 Disciples See the Cursed Fig Tree

Matthew 21:20b; Mark 11:20-26

Early next morning, as they walked along the road, they saw the fig tree. It was dead all the way down to its roots.

The disciples saw this and were astounded. Peter remembered what had happened and said to Jesus, "Look, Teacher, the fig tree you cursed has died! How did the fig tree dry up so quickly?" they asked.

Jesus answered them, "Have faith in God. I assure you that whoever tells this hill to get up and throw itself in the sea and does not doubt in his heart, but believes that what he says will happen, it will be done for him.

"For this reason I tell you: When you pray and ask for something, believe that you have received it, and you will be given whatever you ask for. And when you stand and pray, forgive anything you may have against anyone, so that your Father in heaven will forgive the wrongs you have done."

202 Question of Jesus' Authority

Matthew 21:23-27; Mark 11:27-33; Luke 20:1-8

They arrived once again in Jerusalem. As Jesus was walking in the Temple teaching the people and preaching the Good News, the chief priests and the teachers of the Law, together with the elders, came to him and said, "Tell us, what right do you have to do these things? Who gave you such right?"

Jesus answered them, "I will ask you just one question, and if you give me an answer, I will tell you what right I have to do these things. Tell me, where did John's right to baptize come from: was it from God or from human beings?"

They started to argue among themselves, "What shall we say? If we answer, "From God," he will say to us, "Why, then, did you not believe John?" But if we say, "From human beings," we are afraid of what the people might do, because they are all convinced that John was a prophet."

So they answered Jesus, "We don't know where it came from."

And Jesus said to them, "Neither will I tell you, then, by what right I do these things."

203 Parable of the Two Sons

Matthew 21:28-32

"Now, what do you think? There was once a man who had two sons. He went to the older one and said, 'Son, go and work in the vineyard today.'

"'I don't want to,' he answered, but later he changed his mind and went. Then the father went to the other son and said the same thing.

"'Yes, sir,' he answered, but he did not go. Which one of the two did what his father wanted?"

"The older one," they answered.

So Jesus said to them, "I tell you: the tax collectors and the prostitutes are going into the Kingdom of God ahead of you. For John the Baptist came to you showing you the right path to take, and you would not believe him; but the tax collectors and the prostitutes believed him.

"Even when you saw this, you did not later change your minds and believe him."

204 Parable of the Tenants

Matthew 21:33-46; Mark 12:1-12; Luke 20:9-20a

"Listen to another parable," Jesus said. "There was once a landowner who planted a vineyard, put a fence round it, dug a hole for the wine press, and built a watchtower.

Then he rented the vineyard to tenants and left home on a trip.

"When the time came to gather the grapes, he sent a slave to the tenants to receive from them his share of the harvest. The tenants grabbed the slave, beat him, and sent him back without a thing. Then the owner sent another slave; the tenants beat him over the head and treated him shamefully.

"Again the man sent other slaves, more than the first time, and the tenants treated them the same way, beating some and killing others. The only one left to send was the man's own dear son. Then the owner of the vineyard said, "What shall I do? I will send my own dear son; surely they will respect him!"

"But when the tenants saw the son they said to themselves, "This is the owner's son. Come on, let's kill him, and we will get his property!" So they grabbed him, threw him out of the vineyard, and killed him.

"Now, when the owner of the vineyard comes, what will he do to those tenants?" Jesus asked.

"He will come and kill those men, and turn the vineyard over to other tenants, who will give him his share of the harvest at the right time."

When the people heard this they said, "Surely not!"

Jesus looked at them and asked. "Haven't you ever read what the scriptures say? What, then, does this scripture mean?

'The stone which the builders rejected as worthless turned out to be the most important of all. This was done by the Lord; what a wonderful sight it is!

"'Everyone who falls on that stone will be cut to pieces; and if that stone falls on someone, that person will be crushed to dust.'

"And so I tell you," added Jesus, "the Kingdom of God will be taken away from you and given to a people who will produce the proper fruits."

The Jewish leaders, the chief priests and the Pharisees heard Jesus' parables and knew that he was talking about them, so they tried to arrest him on the spot.

But they were afraid of the crowds, who considered Jesus to be a prophet, so they left him and went away. They looked for an opportunity.

205 Question re Paying Taxes

Matthew 22:15-22; Mark 12:13-17; Luke 20:20b-26

Some Pharisees and some members of Herod's party bribed some men to pretend they were sincere, and they sent them to trap Jesus with questions, so they could hand him over to the authority and power of the Roman Governor.

These spies said to Jesus, "Teacher, we know that what you say and teach is right.

"We know that you tell the truth, without worrying about what people think. You pay no attention to a man's status, but teach the truth about God's will for people. Tell us, is it against our Law to pay taxes to the Roman Emperor? Should we pay them or not?"

Jesus, however, was aware of their evil plan, and so he said, "You hypocrites! Why are you trying to trap me? Show me a silver coin for paying the tax!"

They brought him the coin and he asked them, "Whose face and name are these on it?"

"The Emperor's," they answered.

So Jesus said to them, "Well, then, pay to the Emperor what belongs to the Emperor, and pay to God what belongs to God."

There before the people they could not catch him in a thing, so they kept quiet, amazed at his answer. They left him and went away.

206 Marriage at Resurrection

Matthew. 22:23-33' Mark 12:18-27; Luke 20:27-40

That same day some Sadducees, who say that people will not rise from death, came to Jesus and said, "Teacher, Moses wrote this law for us: 'If a man dies and leaves a wife but no children, that man's brother must marry the widow so they can have children who will be considered the dead man's children.' Now, there were seven brothers who used to live here. The oldest got married and died without having children, so he left his widow to his brother.

"Then the second one married the woman, and he died without having children. The same thing happened to the third brother, and then to the rest: all seven brothers married the woman and died without having children. Last of all, the woman died.

"Now, when all the dead rise to life on the day of resurrection, whose wife will she be? All seven of them had married her."

Jesus answered them, "How wrong you are! And do you know why? It is because you don't know the Scriptures or God's power. The men and women of this age marry, but the men and women who are worthy to rise from death and live in the age to come will not then marry.

"They will be like angels and cannot die. They are the children of God, because they have risen from death.

"And Moses clearly proves that the dead are raised to life. Haven't you ever read in the book of Moses the passage about the burning bush?

"There it is written that God said to Moses, 'I am the God of Abraham, the God of Isaac, and the God of Jacob.' He is the God of the living, not of the dead, for to him all are alive. You are completely wrong!"

Some of the teachers of the Law spoke up, "A good answer, Teacher!" For they did not dare ask him any more questions. When the crowds heard this they were amazed at his teaching.

207 Great Commandment

Matthew 22:34-40; Mark 12:28-34

When the Pharisees heard that Jesus had silenced the Sadducees, they came together, and one of them, a teacher of the Law, was there who heard the discussion. He saw that Jesus had given the Sadducees a good answer, so he came to trap him with a question. "Teacher," he asked, "which commandment is the most important of all in the Law?"

Jesus replied, "The most important one is this: 'Listen, Israel! The Lord our God is the only Lord. Love the Lord your God with all your heart, with all your soul, with all your mind, and with all your strength.' This is the greatest and most important commandment.

"The second most important commandment is this: 'Love your neighbor as you love yourself.' The whole law of Moses and the teachings of the prophets depend on these two commandments. There is no other commandment more important than these two."

The teacher of the Law said to Jesus, "Well done, Teacher! It is true, as you say, that only the Lord is God and that there is no other god but he. And you must love God with all your heart and with all your mind and with all your strength; and you must love your neighbor as you love yourself. It is more important to obey these two commandments than to offer on the altar animals and other sacrifices to God."

Jesus noticed how wise his answer was, and so he told him, "You are not far from the Kingdom of God."

After this nobody dared to ask Jesus any more questions.

208 Question about the Messiah

Matthew 22:41-46; Mark 12:35-37a; Luke 20:41-44

As Jesus was teaching in the Temple, some Pharisees gathered together. Jesus asked them, "What do you think about the Messiah? Whose descendant is he?"

"He is David's descendant," they answered.

"Why, then," Jesus asked, "did the Spirit inspire David to call him 'Lord?' For David himself says in the book of Psalms:

'The Lord said to my Lord: Sit here at my right side until I put your enemies as a footstool under your feet.' Psalm 110:1

"If, then, David called him 'Lord,' how can the Messiah be David's descendant?"

No one was able to give Jesus any answer.

209 Jesus Warns Against the Teachers of the Law and Pharisees

Matthew 23:1-12; Mark 12:37b-40; Luke 20:45-47

A large crowd was listening to Jesus gladly.

Then Jesus spoke to the crowds and to his disciples.

As all the people listened to him, Jesus said, "Be on your guard against the teachers of the Law, who like to walk around in their long robes and love to be greeted with respect in the marketplace; who choose the reserved seats in the synagogues and the best places at feasts; who take advantage of widows and rob them of their homes, and then make a show of saying long prayers! Their punishment will be all the worse!

"The teachers of the Law and the Pharisees are the authorized interpreters of Moses' Law. So you must obey and follow everything they tell you to do; do not, however, imitate their actions, because they don't practice what they preach. They tie onto people's backs loads that are heavy and hard to carry, yet they aren't willing even to lift a finger to help them carry those loads. They do everything so people will see them. Look at the straps with scripture verses on them which they wear on their foreheads and arms, and notice how large they are. Notice also how long are the tassels of their cloaks!

"They love to have people call them 'Teacher.' You must not be called 'Teacher,' because you are all equal and have only one Teacher.

"And you must not call anyone here on earth 'Father,' because you have only the one Father in heaven.

"Nor should you be called 'Leader,' because your one and only leader is the Messiah.

"The greatest one among you must be your servant. Whoever makes himself great will be humbled, and whoever humbles himself will be made great."

210 The Widow's Offering

Mark 12:41-44; Luke 21:1-4

As Jesus sat near the Temple treasury, he watched the people as they dropped in their money. Many rich men dropped in a lot of money; then a poor widow came along and dropped in two little copper coins, worth about a penny.

He called his disciples together and said to them, "I tell you that this poor widow put more in the offering box than all the others. For the others put in what they had to spare of their riches; but she, poor as she is, put in all that she had; she gave all she had to live on."

211 Jesus' Love for Jerusalem

Matthew 23:37-39; Luke 13:34-35

"Jerusalem, Jerusalem! You kill the prophets, you stone the messengers God has sent you! How many times I wanted to put my arms around all your people, just as a hen gathers her chicks under her wings, but you would not let me! And so your Temple will be abandoned. From now on I assure you that you will not see me again until the time comes when you say, 'God bless him who comes in the name of the Lord.'"

212 Jesus Speaks of the Destruction of the Temple

Matthew 24:1-2; Mark 13:1-2; Luke 21-5-6

Some of the disciples were talking about the Temple, how beautiful it looked with its fine stones and the gifts offered to God.

Jesus left and was going away from the Temple when his disciples came to him to call his attention to its buildings. One of his disciples said, "Look, Teacher! What wonderful stones and buildings!"

"Yes," he said, "You see these great buildings? You may well look at all these. I tell you this: the time will come when not a single stone here will be left in its place, every one of them will be thrown down." FP

INSIGHT: *The actual destruction of the Temple and all Jerusalem took place in 70 AD when the city was besieged by Titus, thus fulfilling this prophecy of Jesus.*

213 Troubles and Persecutions

Matthew 24:3-14; Mark 13:3-13; Luke 21:7-19

As Jesus sat on the Mount of Olives, across from the Temple, Peter, James, John, and Andrew came to him in private. "Teacher," they asked, "tell us when all this will be and tell us what will happen to show that the time has come for all these things to take place, that it is the time for your coming and the end of the age."

Jesus answered, "Watch out, and do not let anyone fool you. Many men, claiming to speak for me, will come and say, 'I am the Messiah!' and, 'The time has come,' and they will fool many people. But don't follow them. Don't be afraid when you hear of wars and revolutions; don't be troubled when you hear the noise of battles close by and news of battles far away. Such things must happen first, but they do not mean that the end is near or has come.

"Countries will fight each other, kingdoms will attack one another. There will be terrible earthquakes, famines, and plagues everywhere; there will be strange and terrifying things coming from the sky. All these things are like the first pains of childbirth.

"Before all these things take place, however, you will be arrested and persecuted. You yourselves must watch out.

"You will be arrested and taken to court. You will be handed over to be tried in synagogues and be put in prison. You will be beaten in the synagogues, handed over to be punished and be put to death. You will be brought before kings and rulers for my sake. This will be your chance to tell the Good News.

"But before the end comes, the gospel must first be preached to all peoples. And when you are arrested and taken to court, make up your minds ahead of time not to worry about how you will defend yourselves.

"When the time comes, say whatever is then given to you. I will give you such words and wisdom that none of your enemies will be able to refute or contradict what you say. For the words you speak will not be yours; they will come from the Holy Spirit.

"You will be handed over by your parents, your brothers, your relatives, and your friends; and some of you will be put to death. Men will hand over their own brothers to be put to death; and fathers will do the same to their children. Children will turn against their parents and have them put to death.

"Everyone will hate you because of me. Many will give up their faith at that time; they will betray one another and hate one another. Then many false prophets will appear and fool many people. Such will be the spread of evil that many people's love will grow cold.

"But whoever holds out to the end will be saved. But not a single hair from your heads will be lost. Stand firm, and you will save yourselves. And this Good News about the Kingdom will be preached through all the world for a witness to all people; and then the end will come."

214 The Awful Horror

Matthew 24:15-28; Mark 13:14-23; Luke 21:20-24; 17:20-25

"You will see 'The Awful Horror,' of which the prophet Daniel spoke. standing in the holy place where he should not be."

"When you see Jerusalem surrounded by armies, then you will know that it will soon be destroyed.

"Then those who are in Judea must run away to the hills. Someone who is on the roof of a house must not take the time to go down and get any belongings from the house to take along. Someone who is in the field must not go back to the house for a cloak. Those who are in the city must leave, and those who are out in the country must not go into the city.

"For those will be 'The Days of Punishment,' to make come true all that the Scriptures say. How terrible it will be in those days for women who are pregnant and for mothers with little babies. Pray to God that you will not have to run away during the winter or on a Sabbath!

"For the trouble of those days will be far worse than any the world has ever known from the very beginning when God created the world until the present time. Nor will there be anything like it again. But the Lord has reduced the number of those days; if he had not, nobody would survive. For the sake of those chosen people, however, he has reduced those days.

"Terrible distress will come upon this land, and God's punishment will fall on this people. Some will be killed by the sword, and others will be taken as prisoners to all countries; and the heathen will trample over Jerusalem until their time is up."

Some Pharisees asked Jesus when the Kingdom of God would come. His answer was, "The Kingdom of God does not come in such a way as to be seen.

No one will say, 'Look, here it is!' or, 'There it is!'; because the Kingdom of God is within you."

Then he said to the disciples, "The time will come when you will wish you could see one of the days of the Son of Man, but you will not see it. Then, if anyone says to you, 'Look, here is the Messiah!' or, 'Look, there he is!', do not believe him. Or, if people should tell you, 'Look, he is out in the desert!', don't go there; or if they say, 'Look, he is hiding here!', don't believe it.

"For false Messiahs and false prophets will appear. They will perform great miracles and wonders in order to deceive even God's chosen people, if possible. Be on your guard!

" I have told you everything ahead of time.

"For the Son of Man will come like the lightning which flashes across the whole sky from the east to the west. But first he must suffer much and be rejected by the people of this day."

215 Coming of the Son of Man

Matthew 24:29-31; Mark 13:24-27; Luke 21:25-28

"Soon after the trouble of those days, the sun will grow dark, the moon will no longer shine, the stars will fall from heaven, and the powers in space will be driven from their courses. On earth whole countries will be in despair, afraid of the roar of the sea and the raging tides. People will faint from fear as they wait for what is coming over the whole earth.

"Then the sign of the Son of Man will appear in the sky; and all the peoples of the earth will weep as they see the Son of Man coming on the clouds of heaven with power and great glory.

"When these things begin to happen, stand up and raise your heads, because your salvation is near. The great trumpet will sound, and he will send the angels out to the four corners of the earth to gather God's chosen people from one end of the world to the other."

216 Lesson of the Fig Tree

Matthew 24:32-35; Mark 13:28-31; Luke 21:25-28

Then Jesus told them this parable. "Think of the fig tree and all the other trees. Let the fig tree teach you a lesson. When its branches become green and tender and it starts putting out leaves, you know that summer is near.

"In the same way, when you see these things happening, you will know that the time is near, ready to begin, that the Kingdom of God is about to come. Remember that all these things will happen before the people now living have all died. Heaven and earth will pass away, but my words will never pass away."

217 No One Knows the Day and Hour

Matthew 24:36-44; Mark 13:32-37; Luke 21:34-38; 17:26-37

"Be careful not to let yourselves become occupied with too much feasting and drinking and with the worries of this life, or that Day may suddenly catch you like a trap.

"For it will come upon all people everywhere on earth. Be on watch and pray always that you will have the strength to go safely through all those things that will happen and to stand before the Son of Man.

"No one knows, however, when that day and hour will come, neither the angels in heaven nor the Son; only the Father knows. Be on watch, be alert, for you do not know when the time will come. It will be like a man who goes away from home on a trip and leaves his servants in charge, after giving to each one his own work to do and after telling the doorkeeper to keep watch.

"Watch, then, because you do not know when the master of the house is coming, it might be in the evening or at midnight or before dawn or at sunrise. If he comes suddenly, he must not find you asleep. What I say to you, then, I say to all: Watch!

"The coming of the Son of Man will be like what happened in the time of Noah. In the days before the flood people ate and drank, men and women married, up to the very day Noah went into the boat; yet they did not realize what was happening until the flood came and swept them all away.

"It will be as it was in the time of Lot. Everybody kept on eating and drinking, buying and selling, planting and building. On the day Lot left Sodom, fire and sulphur rained down from heaven and killed them all. That is how it will be on the day the Son of Man is revealed.

"On that day the someone who is on the roof of a house must not go down into the house to get his belongings; in the same way anyone who is out in the field must not go back to the house. Remember Lot's wife!

"Those who try to save their own life will lose it; those who lose their life will save it.

"On that night, I tell you, there will be two people sleeping in the same bed; one will be taken away, the other will be left behind.

"At that time two men will be working in the field: one will be taken away, the other will be left behind. Two women will be at a mill grinding meal: one will be taken away, the other will be left behind."

The disciples asked him, "Where, Lord?"

Jesus answered, "Wherever there is a dead body, the vultures will gather.

"Watch out, then, because you do not know what day your Lord will come. If the owner of a house knew the time when the thief would come, you can be sure that he would stay awake and not let the thief break into his house. So then, you also must always be ready, because the Son of Man will come at an hour when you are not expecting him."

218 Parable of the Ten Girls

Matthew 25:1-13

"At that time the Kingdom of heaven will be like this:

"Once there were ten young women who took their oil lamps and went out to meet the bridegroom.

Five of them were foolish, and the other five were wise. The foolish ones took their lamps but did not take any extra oil with them, while the wise ones took containers full of oil for their lamps. The bridegroom was late in coming, so the girls began to nod and fall asleep.

"It was already midnight when the cry rang out, 'Here is the bridegroom! Come and meet him!' The ten girls woke up and trimmed their lamps.

"Then the foolish ones said to the wise ones, 'Let us have some of your oil, because our lamps are going out.' 'No, indeed,' the wise ones answered, 'there is not enough for you and for us. Go to the store and buy some for yourselves.'

"So the foolish girls went off to buy some oil, and while they were gone, the bridegroom arrived. The five girls who were ready went in with him to the wedding feast, and the door was closed.

"Later the other girls arrived. 'Sir, sir! Let us in!' they cried out.

"'Certainly not! I don't know you,' the bridegroom answered."

And Jesus concluded, "Watch out, then, because you do not know the day or the hour."

219 The Parable of the Gold Coins

Matthew 25:14-30; Luke 19:11-27

While the people were listening to this, Jesus continued and told them a parable. He was now almost at Jerusalem, and they supposed that the Kingdom of God was just about to appear. So he said, "At that time the Kingdom of heaven will be like this:

"There was once a man of high rank who was going to a country far away to be made king, after which he planned to come back home.

"Before he left, he called his servants and put them in charge of his property.

"He gave to each one according to his ability: to one he gave five thousand gold coins, to another he gave two thousand, and to another he gave one thousand. He told them, 'See what you can earn with this while I am gone.'

"Then he left on his trip. Now, his own people hated him, and so they sent messengers after him to say, 'We don't want this man to be our king.'

"The servant who had received five thousand coins went at once and invested his money and earned another five thousand. In the same way the servant who had received two thousand coins earned another two thousand.

"But the servant who had received one thousand coins went off, dug a hole in the ground, and hid his master's money.

"The man was made king. After a long time the master of those servants came back and settled accounts with them.

"At once he ordered his servants to appear before him, in order to find out how much they had earned.

"The servant who had received five thousand coins came in and handed over the other five thousand. 'You gave me five thousand coins, sir,' he said. 'Look! Here are another five thousand that I have earned.' 'Well done, you good and faithful servant!' said his master. 'You have been faithful in managing small amounts, so I will put you in charge of large amounts and in charge of ten cities. Come on in and share my happiness!'

"Then the servant who had been given two thousand coins came in and said, 'You gave me two thousand coins, sir. Look! Here are another two thousand that I have earned.' 'Well done, you good and faithful servant!' said his master. 'You have been faithful in managing small amounts so I will put you in charge of large amounts and in charge of five cities.' Come on in and share my happiness!'

"Then the servant who had received one thousand coins came in and said, 'Sir, I was afraid of you, because you are a hard man. You reap harvests where you did not plant, and gather crops where you did not scatter seed. I was afraid, so I went off and hid your money in the ground, in a handkerchief. Look! Here is what belongs to you.'

"'You bad and lazy servant!' his master said. 'I will use your own words to condemn you! You knew, did you, that I reap harvests where I did not plant, and gather crops where I did not scatter seed?

"Well, then, why didn't you put my money in the bank'? Then I would have received it back with interest when I returned. Then he said to those standing there, 'Take the money away from him and give it to the one who has ten thousand coins.'

"But they said to him, 'Sir, he already has ten thousand coins.'

"'I tell you,' he replied, 'to every person who has something, even more will be given, and he will have more than enough; but the person who has nothing, even the little he has will be taken away from him. As for this useless servant, throw him outside in the darkness; there he will cry and gnash his teeth.

"Now, as for these enemies of mine who did not want me to be their king, bring them here and kill them in my presence!'"

220 The Final Judgment

Matthew 25:31-46

"When the Son of Man comes as King and all the angels with him, he will sit on his royal throne, and the people of all the nations will be gathered before him. Then he will divide them into two groups, just as a shepherd separates his sheep from the goats.

"He will put the righteous people at his right and the others at his left.

"Then the King will say to the people on his right, 'Come, you that are blessed by my Father! Come and possess the kingdom which has been prepared for you ever since the creation of the world. I was hungry and you fed me, thirsty and you gave me drink; I was a stranger and you received me in your homes, naked and you clothed me; I was sick and you took care of me, in prison and you visited me?

"The righteous will then answer him , 'When, Lord, did we ever see you hungry and feed you, or thirsty and give you a drink? When did we ever see you a stranger and welcome you in our homes, or naked and clothe you? When did we ever see you sick or in prison, and visit you?'

"The King will reply, 'I tell you, whenever you did this for one of the least important of these brothers of mine, you did it for me!'

"Then he will say to those on his left, 'Away from me, you that are under God's curse! Away to the eternal fire which has been prepared for the Devil and his angels! I was hungry but you would not feed me, thirsty but you would not give me drink; I was a stranger but you would not welcome me in your homes, naked but you would not clothe me; I was sick and in prison but you would not take care of me.'

"Then they will answer him, 'When, Lord, did we ever see you hungry or thirsty or a stranger or naked or sick or in prison, and we would not help you?'

"Then the King will reply, 'I tell you, whenever you refused to help one of these least important ones, you refused to help me.' These, then, will be sent off to eternal punishment; but the righteous will go to eternal life."

221 Plot Against Jesus

Matthew 26:1-5; Mark 14:1-2; Luke 22:1-2

When Jesus had finished teaching all these things, he said to his disciples, "In two days, as you know, it will be the Passover Festival, and the Son of Man will be handed over to be crucified."

Then the chief priests and the Jewish elders met together in the palace of Caiaphas, the High Priest, and made plans to arrest Jesus secretly and put him to death.

"We must not do it during the festival," they said, "or the people will riot."

222 Jesus Anointed at Bethany

Matthew 26:6-13; Mark 14:3-9; Luke 7:36-50

Jesus was in Bethany at the house of Simon, a Pharisee, a man who suffered from a dreaded skin disease. Jesus went to his house and sat down to eat. In that town was a woman who lived a sinful life.

She heard that Jesus was eating in the Pharisee's house, so she brought an alabaster jar full of expensive perfume made of pure nard.

She broke the jar and poured the perfume on Jesus' head. She stood behind Jesus, by his feet, crying and wetting his feet with her tears. Then she dried his feet with her hair, kissed them, and poured the perfume on them.

When the Pharisee saw this, he said to himself, "If this man really were a prophet, he would know who this woman is who is touching him; he would know what kind of sinful life she lives!"

Jesus spoke up and said to him, "Simon, I have something to tell you."

"Yes, Teacher," he said, "tell me."

"There were two men who owed money to a moneylender," Jesus began. "One owed him five hundred silver coins, and the other owed him fifty.

" Neither of them could pay him back, so he canceled the debts of both. Which one, then, will love him more?"

"I suppose," answered Simon, "that it would be the one who was forgiven more."

"You are right," said Jesus. Then he turned to the woman and said to Simon, "Do you see this woman? I came into your home, and you gave me no water for my feet, but she has washed my feet with her tears and dried them with her hair.

"You did not welcome me with a kiss, but she has not stopped kissing my feet since I came. You provided no olive oil for my head, but she has covered my feet with perfume. I tell you, then, the great love she has shown proves that her many sins have been forgiven. But whoever has been forgiven little shows only a little love."

Then Jesus said to the woman, "Your sins are forgiven."

The others sitting at the table began to say to themselves, "Who is this, who even forgives sins?"

But Jesus said to the woman, "Your faith has saved you, go in peace."

The disciples and some of the people there became angry and said to one another, "What was the use of wasting the perfume? It could have been sold for more than three hundred silver coins and the money given to the poor!" And they criticized her harshly.

Jesus knew what they were saying, and so he said to them, "Leave her alone! Why are you bothering this woman? It is a fine and beautiful thing that she has done for me. You will always have poor people with you, and any time you want to, you can help them. But you will not always have me. She did what she could; she poured perfume on my body to prepare it ahead of time for burial. Now, I assure you that wherever this gospel is preached all over the world, what she has done will be told in memory of her."

223 Judas Agrees to Betray Jesus

Matthew 26:14-16; Mark 14:10-11; Luke 22:3-6

Then Satan entered into Judas, called Iscariot, who was one of the twelve disciples. So Judas went off and spoke with the chief priests and the officers of the Temple guard and asked, "What will you give me if I betray Jesus to you?"

"They were pleased to hear what he had to say. They counted out thirty silver coins and gave them to him. Judas agreed to it and started looking for a good chance to hand Jesus over to them without the people knowing about it.

224 Preparation for Passover Meal

Matthew 26:17-19; Mark 14:12-16; Luke 22:7-13

The day came during the Festival of Unleavened Bread when the lambs for the Passover meal were to be killed. Jesus sent Peter and John with these instructions, "Go and get the Passover meal ready for us to eat."

"Where do you want us to get it ready for you?" they asked him.

He answered, "As you go into the city, a man carrying a jar of water will meet you.

"Follow him into the house that he enters, and say to the owner of the house: 'The Teacher says to you, Where is the room where my disciples and I will eat the Passover meal?' He will show you a large furnished room upstairs, where you will get everything ready."

They went off and found everything just as Jesus had told them; and they prepared the Passover meal.

225 Jesus Washes Disciples' Feet

Luke 22:14; John 13:1-20

It was now the day before the Passover Festival. Jesus knew that the hour had come for him to leave this world and go to the Father. He had always loved those in the world who were his own, and he loved them to the very end.

When the hour came, Jesus took his place at the table with the apostles.

The Devil had already put into the heart of Judas, the son of Simon Iscariot, the thought of betraying Jesus.

Jesus knew that the Father had given him complete power; he knew that he had come from God and was going to God. So he rose from the table, took off his outer garment, and tied a towel round his waist. Then he poured some water into a washbasin and began to wash the disciples' feet and dry them with the towel round his waist. He came to Simon Peter, who said to him, "Are you going to wash my feet, Lord?"

Jesus answered him, "You do not understand now what I am doing, but you will understand later."

Peter declared, "Never at any time will you wash my feet!"

"If I do not wash your feet," Jesus answered, "you will no longer be my disciple."

Simon Peter answered, "Lord, do not wash only my feet, then! Wash my hands and head, too!"

Jesus said, "Those who have taken a bath are completely clean and do not have to wash themselves, except for their feet. All of you are clean, all except one." (Jesus already knew who was going to betray him; that is why he said, "All of you, except one, are clean.")

After Jesus had washed their feet, he put his outer garment back on and returned to his place at the table.

"Do you understand what I have just done to you?" he asked.

"You call me Teacher and Lord, and it is right that you do so, because that is what I am. I, your Lord and Teacher, have just washed your feet. You, then, should wash one another's feet. I have set an example for you, so that you will do just what I have done for you.

"I am telling you the truth: no slaves are greater than their master, and no messengers are greater than the one who sent them.

"Now that you know this truth; how happy you will be if you put it into practice!

"I am not talking about all of you; I know those I have chosen. But the scripture must come true that says,

'The man who shared my food turned against me.' Psalm 41:9

"I tell you this now before it happens, so that when it does happen, you will believe that 'I Am Who I Am'. I am telling you the truth: whoever receives anyone I send receives me also; and whoever receives me receives him who sent me."

226 Predicts His Betrayals

Matthew 26:20-25; Mark 14:17-21; Luke 22:21-23; John 13:21-35

After Jesus had said this, he was deeply troubled and declared openly, "I am telling you the truth: one of you is going to betray me. But, look! The one who betrays me is here at the table with me! The Son of Man will die as God has decided, but how terrible for that man who betrays him! It would have been better for that man if he had never been born!"

The disciples looked at one another, completely puzzled about whom he meant.

Then they began to ask among themselves which one of them it could be who was going to do this. The disciples were upset and began to ask him, one after the other, "Surely you don't mean me, do you?"

One of the disciples, the one whom Jesus loved, was sitting next to Jesus. Simon Peter motioned to him and said, "Ask him whom he is talking about."

So that disciple moved closer to Jesus' side and asked, "Who is it, Lord?"

Jesus answered, "I will dip the bread in the sauce and give it to him; he is the man." So he took a piece of bread, dipped it, and gave it to Judas, the son of Simon Iscariot.

Judas, the traitor, spoke up. "Surely, Teacher, you don't mean me?" he asked.

Jesus answered, "So you say."

As soon as Judas took the bread, Satan entered into him. Jesus said to him, "Hurry and do what you must!" None of the others at the table understood why Jesus said this to him. Since Judas was in charge of the money bag, some of the disciples thought that Jesus had told him to go and buy what they needed for the festival, or to give something to the poor.

Judas accepted the bread and went out at once. It was night.

After Judas had left, Jesus said, "Now the Son of Man's glory is revealed; now God's glory is revealed through him. And if God's glory is revealed through him, then God will reveal the glory of the Son of Man in himself, and he will do so at once.

My children, I shall not be with you very much longer. You will look for me; but I tell you now what I told the Jewish authorities, 'You cannot go where I am going.' And now I give you a new commandment: love one another. As I have loved you, so you must love one another.

"If you have love for one another, then everyone will know that you are my disciples."

227 The Lord's Supper

Matthew 26:26-29; Mark 14:22-25; Luke 22:15-20

He said to them, "I have wanted so much to eat this Passover meal with you before I suffer! For I tell you, I will never eat it until it is given its full meaning in the Kingdom of God."

While they were eating, Jesus took a piece of bread, gave a prayer of thanks, broke it, and gave it to his disciples. "Take and eat it," he said; "this is my body, which is given for you. Do this in memory of me."

Then he took a cup, gave thanks to God, and said, "Take this and share it among yourselves." "Drink it, all of you," he said, "this is my blood, which seals God's covenant, my blood poured out for many for the forgiveness of sins." He handed it to them; and they all drank from it. "I tell you, I will never again drink this wine until the day I drink the new wine with you in my Father's Kingdom."

228 Argument about Greatness

Luke 22:24-30

An argument broke out among the disciples as to which one of them should be thought of as the greatest. Jesus said to them, "The kings of the pagans have power over their people, and the rulers claim the title 'Friends of the People.'

"But this is not the way it is with you; rather, the greatest one among you must be like the youngest, and the leader must be like the servant. Who is greater, the one who sits down to eat or the one who serves? The one who sits down, of course. But I am among you as one who serves.

"You have stayed with me all through my trials; and just as my Father has given me the right to rule, so I will give you the same right. You will eat and drink at my table in my Kingdom, and you will sit on thrones to rule over the twelve tribes of Israel."

229 Jesus Predicts Peter's Denial

Matthew 26:31-35; Mark 14:27-31; Luke 22:31-34; John 13:36-38

Then Jesus said to them, "This very night all of you will run away and leave me, for the scripture says, 'God will kill the shepherd and the sheep of the flock will be scattered.' But after I am raised to life, I will go to Galilee ahead of you."

"Where are you going, Lord?" Simon Peter asked him.

"You cannot follow me now where I am going," answered Jesus; "but later you will follow me. Simon, Simon! Listen! Satan has received permission to test all of you, to separate the good from the bad, as a farmer separates the wheat from the chaff. But I have prayed for you, Simon, that your faith will not fail. And when you turn back to me, you must strengthen your brothers."

"Lord, why can't I follow you now?" asked Peter. "I am ready to go to prison with you and to die with you! I will never leave you, even though all the rest do!"

Jesus answered, "Are you really ready to die for me? I am telling you the truth: before the rooster crows two times tonight, you will say three times that you do not know me."

Peter answered even more strongly, "I will never say that, even if I have to die with you!"

And all the other disciples said the same thing.

230 Jesus the Way to the Father

John 14:1-14

"Do not be worried and upset," Jesus told them. "Believe in God, and believe also in me. There are many rooms in my Father's house, and I am going to prepare a place for you. I would not tell you this if it were not so. And after I go and prepare a place for you, I will come back and take you to myself, so that you will be where I am. You know the way that leads to the place where I am going."

Thomas said to him, "Lord, we do not know where you are going; so how can we know the way to get there?"

Jesus answered him, "I am the way, the truth, and the life; no one goes to the Father except by me.

Now that you have known me," he said to them, "you will know my Father also, and from now on you do know him and you have seen him."

Philip said to him, "Lord, show us the Father; that is all we need."

Jesus answered, "For a long time I have been with you all; yet you do not know me, Philip? Whoever has seen me has seen the Father. Why, then, do you say, 'Show us the Father?' Do you not believe, Philip, that I am in the Father and the Father is in me?

"The words that I have spoken to you," Jesus said to his disciples, "do not come from me. The Father, who remains in me, does his own work.

"Believe me when I say that I am in the Father and the Father is in me. If not, believe because of the things I do. I am telling you the truth: those who believe in me will do what I do? Yes, they will do even greater things, because I am going to the Father.

"And I will do whatever you ask for in my name, so that the Father's glory will be shown through the Son.

"If you ask me for anything in my name, I will do it."

231 Promise of the Holy Spirit

Matthew 26:30; Mark 14:26; John 14:15-31

"If you love me, you will obey my commandments. I will ask the Father, and he will give you another Helper, who will stay with you forever. He is the Spirit, who reveals the truth about God. The world cannot receive him, because it cannot see him or know him. But you know him, because he remains with you and is in you.

"When I go, you will not be left all alone; I will come back to you. In a little while the world will see me no more, but you will see me; and because I live, you also will live. When that day comes, you will know that I am in my Father and that you are in me, just as I am in you.

"Those who accept my commandments and obey them are the ones who love me. My Father will love those who love me; I too will love them and reveal myself to them."

Judas (not Judas Iscariot) said, "Lord, how can it be that you will reveal yourself to us and not to the world?"

Jesus answered him, "Those who love me will obey my teaching. My Father will love them, and my Father and I will come to them and live with them. Those who do not love me do not obey my teaching.

And the teaching you have heard is not mine, but comes from the Father, who sent me.

"I have told you this while I am still with you. The Helper, the Holy Spirit, whom the Father will send in my name, will teach you everything and make you remember all that I have told you.

"Peace is what I leave with you; it is my own peace that I give you. I do not give it as the world does. Do not be worried and upset; do not be afraid. You heard me say to you, 'I am leaving, but I will come back to you.'

"If you loved me, you would be glad that I am going to the Father, for he is greater than I.

"I have told you this now before it all happens, so that when it does happen, you will believe. I cannot talk with you much longer, because the ruler of this world is coming. He has no power over me, but the world must know that I love the Father; that is why I do everything as he commands me.

"Come, let us go from this place." Then they sang a hymn and went out to the Mount of Olives.

232 Jesus the Real Vine

John 15:1-17

"I am the real vine, and my Father is the gardener. He breaks off every branch in me that does not bear fruit, and he prunes every branch that does bear fruit, so that it will be clean and bear more fruit. You have been made clean already by the teaching I have given to you.

"Remain united to me, and I will remain united to you. A branch cannot bear fruit by itself; it can do so only if it remains in the vine. In the same way you cannot bear fruit unless you remain in me.

"I am the vine, and you are the branches. Those who remain in me, and I in them, will bear much fruit; for you can do nothing without me. Those who do not remain in me are thrown out like a branch and dry up; such branches are gathered up and thrown into the fire, where they are burned.

"If you remain in me and my words remain in you, then you will ask for anything you wish, and you shall have it. My Father's glory is shown by your bearing much fruit; and in this way you become my disciples. I love you just as the Father loves me; remain in my love. If you obey my commands, you will remain in my love, just as I have obeyed my Father's commands and remain in his love.

"I have told you this so that my joy may be in you and that your joy may be complete. My commandment is this: love one another, just as I love you. The greatest love you can have for your friends is to give your life for them.

"And you are my friends if you do what I command you. I do not call you servants any longer, because servants do not know what their master is doing.

"Instead, I call you friends, because I have told you everything I heard from my Father.

"You did not choose me; I chose you and appointed you to go and bear much fruit, the kind of fruit that endures. And so the Father will give you whatever you ask of him in my name. This, then, is what I command you: love one another."

233 World's Hatred

John 15:18-16:4a

"If the world hates you, just remember that it has hated me first. If you belonged to the world, then the world would love you as its own.

"But I chose you from this world, and you do not belong to it; that is why the world hates you. Remember what I told you: 'Slaves are not greater than their master.' If they persecuted me, they will persecute you too; if they obeyed my teaching, they will obey yours too. But they will do all this to you because you are mine; for they do not know the one who sent me.

"They would not have been guilty of sin if I had not come and spoken to them; as it is, they no longer have any excuse for their sin. Whoever hates me hates my Father also.

"They would not have been guilty of sin if I had not done among them the things that no one else ever did; as it is, they have seen what I did, and they hate both me and my Father.

"This, however, was bound to happen so that what is written in their Law may come true: 'They hated me for no reason at all.'

"The Helper will come - the Spirit, who reveals the truth about God and who comes from the Father. I will send him to you from the Father, and he will speak about me. And you, too, will speak about me, because you have been with me from the very beginning.

"I have told you this, so that you will not give up your faith.

"You will be expelled from the synagogues, and the time will come when those who kill you will think that by doing this they are serving God. People will do these things to you because they have not known either the Father or me. But I have told you this, so that when the time comes for them to do these things, you will remember what I told you."

234 Work of the Holy Spirit

John 16:4b-15

"I did not tell you these things at the beginning, for I was with you. But now I am going to him who sent me, yet none of you asks me where I am going. And now that I have told you, your hearts are full of sadness. But I am telling you the truth: it is better for you that I go away, because if I do not go, the Helper will not come to you. But if I do go away, then I will send him to you.

"And when he comes, he will prove to the people of the world that they are wrong about sin and about what is right and about God's judgment. They are wrong about sin, because they do not believe in me; they are wrong about what is right, because I am going to the Father and you will not see me anymore; and they are wrong about judgment, because the ruler of this world has already been judged.

"I have much more to tell you, but now it would be too much for you to bear. When, however, the Spirit comes, who reveals the truth about God, he will lead you into all the truth. He will not speak on his own authority, but he will speak of what he hears and tell you of things to come. He will give me glory, because he will take what I say and tell it to you. All that my Father has is mine; that is why I said that the Spirit will take what I give him and tell it to you."

235 Sadness and Gladness

John 16:16-24

"In a little while you will not see me anymore, and then a little while later you will see me."

Some of his disciples asked among themselves, "What does this mean?

"He tells us that in a little while we will not see him, and then a little while later we will see him?; and he also says, 'It is because I am going to the Father.' What does this 'a little while' mean? We don't know what he is talking about!"

Jesus knew that they wanted to question him, so he said to them, "I said, 'In a little while you will not see me, and then a little while later you will see me.'

"Is this what you are asking about among yourselves? I am telling you the truth: you will cry and weep, but the world will be glad; you will be sad, but your sadness will turn into gladness.

"When a woman is about to give birth, she is sad because her hour of suffering has come; but when the baby is born, she forgets her suffering, because she is happy that a baby has been born into the world.

"That is how it is with you: now you are sad, but I will see you again, and your hearts will be filled with gladness, the kind of gladness that no one can take away from you.

"When that day comes, you will not ask me for anything. I am telling you the truth: the Father will give you whatever you ask of him in my name. Until now you have not asked for anything in my name; ask and you will receive, so that your happiness may be complete."

236 Victory over the World

John 16:25-33

"I have used figures of speech to tell you of these things. But the time will come when I will not use figures of speech, but will speak to you plainly about the Father. When that day comes, you will ask him in my name; and I do not say that I will ask him on your behalf, for the Father himself loves you. He loves you because you love me and have believed that I came from God.

"I did come from the Father and I came into the world; and now I am leaving the world and going to the Father."

Then his disciples said to him, "Now you are speaking plainly, without using figures of speech. We know now that you know everything; you do not need to have someone ask you questions. This makes us believe that you came from God."

Jesus answered them, "Do you believe now? The time is coming, and is already here, when all of you will be scattered, each of you to your own home, and I will be left all alone. But I am not really alone, because the Father is with me. I have told you this so that you will have peace by being united to me. The world will make you suffer.

But be brave! I have defeated the world!"

237 Jesus Prays for Disciples

John 17:1-26

After Jesus finished saying this, he looked up to heaven and said, "Father, the hour has come. Give glory to your Son, so that the Son may give glory to you. For you gave him authority over all people, so that he might give eternal life to all those you gave him. And eternal life means to know you, the only true God, and to know Jesus Christ, whom you sent. I have shown your glory on earth; I have finished the work you gave me to do. Father! Give me glory in your presence now, the same glory I had with you before the world was made.

"I have made you known to those you gave me out of the world. They belonged to you, and you gave them to me. They have obeyed your word, and now they know that everything you gave me comes from you. I gave them the message that you gave me, and they received it; they know that it is true that I came from you, and they believe that you sent me.

"I pray for them. I do not pray for the world but for those you gave me, se of their message. I pray that they may all be one. Father! May they be in us, just as you are in me and I am in you. May they be one, so that the world will believe that you sent me. I gave them the same glory you gave me, so that they may be one, just as you and I are one: I in them and you in me, so that they may be completely one, in order that the world may know that you sent me and that you love them as you love me.

"Father! You have given them to me, and I want them to be with me where I am, so that they may see my glory, the glory you gave me; for you loved me before the world was made. Righteous Father! The world does not know you, but I know you, and these know that you sent me. I made you known to them, and I will continue to do so, in order that the love you have for me may be in them, and so that I also may be in them."

238 Purse, Bag, and Sword

Luke 22:35-38

Then Jesus asked his disciples, "When I sent you out that time without purse, bag, or shoes, did you lack anything?"

"Not a thing," they answered.

"But now," Jesus said, "whoever has a purse or a bag must take it; and whoever does not have a sword must sell his coat and buy one.

"For I tell you that the scripture which says,

'He shared the fate of criminals', FP Isaiah 53:12

must come true about me, because what was written about me is coming true."

The disciples said, "Look! Here are two swords, Lord!"

"That is enough!" he replied.

239 Jesus Prays in Gethsemane

Matthew 26:36-46; Mark 14:32-42; Luke 22:39-46; John 17:1-24

Jesus left the city and went, as he usually did, across Kidron Brook, to the Mount of Olives ,to a place called Gethsemane. When he arrived at the place, he said to them, "Pray that you will not fall into temptation. Sit here while I go over there and pray." He took with him Peter and the two sons of Zebedee, James and John.

Distress, grief and anguish came over him, and he said to them, "The sorrow in my heart is so great that it almost crushes me. Stay here and keep watch with me."

Then he went off from them about the distance of a stone's throw, and threw himself face downward on the ground, and prayed, "My Father, if it is possible, take this cup of suffering from me! Not my will, however, but your will be done."

An angel from heaven appeared to him and strengthened him. In great anguish he prayed even more fervently; his sweat was like drops of blood falling to the ground.

Then he returned to the three disciples and found them asleep; and he said to Peter, "How is it that you three were not able to keep watch with me for even one hour?" And he said to them, "Keep watch, and pray that you will not fall into temptation. The spirit is willing, but the flesh is weak."

Once more Jesus went away and prayed, "My Father, if this cup of suffering cannot be taken away unless I drink it, your will be done." He returned once more and found the disciples asleep; they could not keep their eyes open.

And they did not know what to say to him.

Again Jesus left them, went away, and prayed the third time, saying the same words. Rising from his prayer, he went back to the disciples and found them asleep, worn out by their grief. He said to them, "Are you still sleeping and resting? Enough! Get up, and pray that you will not fall into temptation. Look! The hour has come for the Son of Man to be handed over to the power of sinful men. Get up, let us go."

There was a garden in that place, and Jesus and his disciples went in.

"Look, here is the man who is betraying me!"

240 Arrest of Jesus

Matthew 26:47-56; Mark 14:43-52; Luke 22:47-53; John 18:1-11

Jesus was still speaking when Judas, one of the twelve disciples, arrived. Judas, the traitor, knew where the garden was, because many times Jesus had met there with his disciples. So Judas went to the garden, taking with him a group of Roman soldiers, and some Temple guards sent by the chief priests and the Pharisees; they were armed and carried lanterns and torches.

The traitor had given the crowd a signal: "The man I kiss is the one you want. Arrest him and take him away under guard."

As soon as Judas arrived he went up to Jesus and said, "Peace be with you, Teacher," and kissed him. But Jesus said, "Judas, is it with a kiss that you betray the Son of Man? Be quick about it, friend!"

Jesus knew everything that was going to happen to him, so he stepped forward and asked them, "Who is it you are looking for?"

"Jesus of Nazareth," they answered.

"I am he," he said.

Judas, the traitor, was standing there with them. When Jesus said to them, "I am he," they moved back and fell to the ground. Again Jesus asked them, "Who is it you are looking for?"

"Jesus of Nazareth," they said.

"I have already told you that I am he," Jesus said. "If, then, you are looking for me, let these others go." (He said this so that what he had said might come true, "Father, I have not lost even one of those you gave me.")

Then they came up, arrested Jesus, and held him tight.

When the disciples who were with Jesus saw what was going to happen, they asked, "Shall we use our swords, Lord?"

Simon Peter, who had a sword drew it and struck the High Priest's slave, cutting off his right ear. The name of the slave was Malchus. Jesus said to Peter,

"Enough of this! Put your sword back in its place! All who take the sword will die by the sword. Don't you know that I could call on my Father for help and at once he would send me more than twelve armies of angels? But in that case, how could the Scriptures come true which say that this is what must happen? Do you think that I will not drink the cup of suffering which my Father has given me?" He touched the man's ear and healed him.

Then Jesus said to the chief priests and the officers of the Temple guard and the elders who had come there to get him, "Did you have to come with swords and clubs to capture me, as though I were an outlaw? Every day I sat down and taught in the Temple, and you did not arrest me. But all this has happened in order to make come true what the prophets wrote in the Scriptures. But this is your hour to act, when the power of darkness rules."

Then all the disciples left him and ran away.

A certain young man, dressed only in a linen cloth, was following Jesus. They tried to arrest him, but he ran away naked, leaving the cloth behind.

241 Jesus Before Annas

John 18:12-14; 19-24

Then the Roman soldiers with their commanding officer and the Jewish guards arrested Jesus, tied him up, and took him first to Annas. He was the father-in-law of Caiaphas, who was High Priest that year.

It was Caiaphas who had advised the Jewish authorities that it was better that one man die for all the people.

The High Priest questioned Jesus about his disciples and about his teaching. Jesus answered, "I have always spoken publicly to everyone; all my teaching was done in the synagogues and in the Temple, where all the people come together.

"I have never said anything in secret. Why, then, do you question me? Question the people who heard me.

"Ask them what I told them - they know what I said."

When Jesus said this, one of the guards there slapped him and said, "How dare you talk like that to the High Priest!"

Jesus answered him, "If I have said anything wrong, tell everyone here what it was. But if I am right in what I have said, why do you hit me?"

Then Annas sent him, still tied up, to Caiaphas the High Priest.

242 Denies Jesus

Matthew 26:69-75; Mark 14:66-72; Luke 22:54-62; John 18:15-18; 25-27

Simon Peter and another disciple followed Jesus.

That other disciple was well known to the High Priest, so he went with Jesus into the courtyard of the High Priest's house, while Peter stayed outside by the gate. Then the other disciple went back out, spoke to the girl at the gate and brought Peter inside.

The girl at the gate said to Peter, "Aren't you also one of the disciples of that man? You, too, were with Jesus of Galilee."

But he denied it in front of them all. "I don't know...I don't understand what you are talking about. Woman, I don't even know Him!" he answered, and went out into the passageway to the entrance of the courtyard. Just then a rooster crowed.

It was cold, so the servants and guards had built a charcoal fire and were standing around it, warming themselves. So Peter went over and stood with them, warming himself.

The servant girl saw him there and began to repeat to the bystanders, "He is one of them! He was with Jesus of Nazareth."

After a little while a man noticed Peter and insisted strongly, "You are one of them, too! After all, the way you speak gives you away!"

Peter denied it and answered, "No, I am not. I swear that I don't know that man!"

One of the High Priest's slaves, a relative of the man whose ear Peter had cut off, spoke up. "Didn't I see you with him in the garden?" he asked.

Then Peter said, "I swear that I am telling the truth! May God punish me if I am not! I do not know the man you are talking about!"

At once, while he was still speaking, a rooster crowed a second time. The Lord turned around and looked straight at Peter and Peter remembered how Jesus had said to him, "Before the rooster crows two times you will say three times that you do not know me."

Peter went out and wept bitterly.

243 Before the Council

Matthew 26:59-66; Mark 14:55-64; Luke 22:63-71

When day came, the elders, the chief priests, and the teachers of the Law met together, and Jesus was brought before the Council.

Peter went into the courtyard and sat down with the guards to see how it would all come out.

The chief priests and the whole council tried to find some false evidence against Jesus in order to put him to death; but they could not find any. Many witnesses told lies against Jesus, but their stories did not agree.

Finally two men stepped up and told this lie against Jesus, "We heard him say, 'I will tear down this Temple which men have made, and after three days I will build one that is not made by men.'" Not even they, however, could make their stories agree.

The High Priest stood up in front of them all and questioned Jesus, "Have you no answer to the accusation they bring against you?"

But Jesus kept quiet and would not say a word. Again the High Priest questioned him, "In the name of the living God I now put you under oath: Are you the Messiah, the Son of the Blessed God?"

He answered, "If I tell you, you will not believe me; and if I ask you a question, you will not answer."

They all said, "Are you, then, the Son of God?"

"I am," answered Jesus, "but I tell all of you: from this time on you will all see the Son of Man seated at the right side of the Almighty and coming on the clouds of heaven!"

At this the High Priest tore his clothes and said, "Blasphemy! We don't need any more witnesses! You have just heard his blasphemy! What do you think? What is your decision?"

They all voted against him: he was guilty and should be put to death.

The men who were guarding Jesus made fun of him and beat him. Some of them began to spit on Jesus, and they blindfolded him and hit him. "Prophesy for us, Messiah! Guess who hit you!" they said. And they said many other insulting things to him. And the guards took him and slapped him.

244 Jesus Taken to Pilate

Matthew 27:1-2; Mark 15:1-5; Luke 23:1-5; John 18:28-38a

Early in the morning all the chief priests and the elders made their plans against Jesus to put him to death. They put him in chains, led him from Caiaphas' house to the governor's palace and handed him over to Pilate, the Roman governor. The Jewish authorities did not go inside the palace, for they wanted to keep themselves ritually clean, in order to be able to eat the Passover meal. So Pilate went outside to them and asked, "What do you accuse this man of?"

Their answer was, "We would not have brought him to you if he had not committed a crime.

We caught this man misleading our people, telling them not to pay taxes to the Emperor and claiming that he himself is the Messiah, a king."

Pilate said to them, "Then you yourselves take him and try him according to your own law."

They replied, "We are not allowed to put anyone to death." (This happened in order to make come true what Jesus had said when he indicated the kind of death he would die.)

Pilate went back into the palace and called Jesus."Are you the king of the Jews?" he asked him.

Jesus answered, "So you say. Does this question come from you or have others told you about me?"

Pilate replied, "Do you think I am a Jew? It was your own people and the chief priests who handed you over to me. What have you done?"

Jesus said, "My kingdom does not belong to this world; if my kingdom belonged to this world, my followers would fight to keep me from being handed over to the Jewish authorities. No, my kingdom does not belong here!"

So Pilate asked him, "Are you a king, then?"

Jesus answered, "You say that I am a king. I was born and came into the world for this one purpose, to speak about the truth. Whoever belongs to the truth listens to me."

"And what is truth?" Pilate asked.

The chief priests were accusing Jesus of many things, so Pilate questioned him again, "Aren't you going to answer? Listen to all their accusations!"

But Jesus refused to answer a single word, with the result that the Governor was greatly surprised."

Then Pilate said to the chief priests and the crowds, "I find no reason to condemn this man."

But they insisted even more strongly, "With his teaching he is starting a riot among the people all through Judea. He began in Galilee and now has come here."

245 Jesus before Herod

Luke 23:6-12

When Pilate heard this he asked, "Is this man a Galilean?" When he learned that Jesus was from the region ruled by Herod, he sent him to Herod, who was also in Jerusalem at that time.

Herod was very pleased when he saw Jesus, because he had heard about him and had been wanting to see him for a long time. He was hoping to see Jesus perform some miracle. So Herod asked Jesus many questions, but Jesus made no answer.

The chief priests and the teachers of the Law stepped forward and made strong accusations against Jesus.

Herod and his soldiers made fun of Jesus and treated him with contempt; then they put a fine robe on him and sent him back to Pilate.

On that very day Herod and Pilate became friends; before this they had been enemies.

246 Jesus Sentenced to Death

Matthew 27:15-31; Mark 15:6-20; Luke 23:13-25; John 18:38b-19:16a

Pilate called together the chief priests, the leaders, and the people, and said to them, "You brought this man to me and said that he was misleading the people. Now, I have examined him here in your presence, and I have not found him guilty of any of the crimes you accuse him of. Nor did Herod find him guilty, for he sent him back to us. There is nothing this man has done to deserve death. So I will have him whipped and let him go."

At every Passover Festival the Roman governor was in the habit of setting free any one prisoner the crowd asked for. At that time there was a well-known prisoner named Jesus Barabbas.

(Barabbas had been put in prison for a riot that had taken place in the city, and for murder.)

Pilate wanted to set Jesus free, so when the crowd gathered, Pilate asked them, "Which one do you want me to set free for you? Jesus Barabbas or Jesus called the Messiah?" He knew very well that the Jewish authorities had handed Jesus over to him because they were jealous.

While Pilate was sitting in the judgment hall, his wife sent him a message: "Have nothing to do with that innocent man, because in a dream last night I suffered much on account of him."

The chief priests and the elders persuaded the crowd to ask Pilate to set Barabbas free and have Jesus put to death. But Pilate asked the crowd, "Which one of these two do you want me to set free for you?"

"Barabbas!" they answered.

"What, then, shall I do with Jesus called the Messiah?" Pilate asked them.

"Crucify him!" they all answered.

But Pilate asked, "What crime has he committed?"

Then they started shouting at the top of their voices, "Crucify him! Set Barabbas free for us!"

Then Pilate's soldiers took Jesus inside the courtyard of the governor's palace, and the whole company gathered around him. They stripped off his clothes and put a scarlet (purple) robe on him.

Then they made a crown out of thorny branches and placed it on his head, and put a stick in his right hand; then they knelt before him and made fun of him. "Long live the King of the Jews!" they said.

They spat on him, and took the stick and hit him over the head.

Pilate went back out once more and said to the crowd, "Look, I will bring him out here to you to let you see that I cannot find any reason to condemn him."

So Jesus came out, wearing the crown of thorns and the purple (scarlet) robe. Pilate said to them, "Look! Here is the man!"

When the chief priests and the Temple guards saw him, they shouted, "Crucify him! Crucify him!"

Pilate said to them, "You take him, then, and crucify him. I find no reason to condemn him."

The crowd answered back, "We have a law that says he ought to die, because he claimed to be the Son of God."

When Pilate heard this, he was even more afraid. He went back into the palace and asked Jesus, "Where do you come from?"

But Jesus did not answer. Pilate said to him, "You will not speak to me? Remember, I have the authority to set you free and also to have you crucified."

Jesus answered, "You have authority over me only because it was given to you by God.

So the man who handed me over to you is guilty of a worse sin."

When Pilate heard this, he tried to find a way to set Jesus free. But the crowd shouted back, "If you set him free, that means that you are not the Emperor's friend! Anyone who claims to be a king is a rebel against the Emperor!"

When Pilate heard these words, he took Jesus outside and sat down on the judge's seat in the place called "The Stone Pavement." (In Hebrew the name is "Gabbatha.") Pilate said to the people, "Here is your king!"

They shouted back, "Kill him! Kill him! Crucify him!"

Pilate asked them," Do you want me to crucify your king?"

The chief priests answered, "The only king we have is the Emperor!"

When Pilate saw it was no use to go on, but that a riot might break out, he took some water, washed his hands in front of the crowd, and said, "I am not responsible for the death of this man! This is your doing!"

The whole crowd answered, "Let the responsibility for his death fall on us and on our children!"

When they had finished, they took the robe off and put his own clothes back on him. Then Pilate handed Jesus over to them to be crucified.

Pilate wanted to please the crowd, so he set Barabbas free for them, the man they wanted, the one who had been put in prison for riot and murder.

247 Death of Judas

Matthew 27:3-10

When Judas, the traitor, learned that Jesus had been condemned, he repented and took back the thirty silver coins to the chief priests and the elders. "I have sinned by betraying an innocent man to death!" he said.

"What do we care about that?" they answered. "That is your business!"

Judas threw the coins down in the Temple and left; then he went off and hanged himself.

The chief priests picked up the coins and said, "This is blood money, and it is against our Law to put it in the Temple treasury."

After reaching an agreement about it, they used the money to buy Potter's Field, as a cemetery for foreigners. That is why that field is called "Field of Blood" to this very day.

Then what the prophet Jeremiah had said came true,

> "They took the thirty silver coins, the amount the people of Israel had agreed to pay for him, and used the money to buy the potter's field, as the Lord commanded me." FP Zechariah 11:12-13

248 Jesus Nailed to the Cross

Matthew 27:32-44; Mark 15:21-32; Luke 23:26-43; John 19:16b-27

So they took charge of Jesus. He went out, carrying his cross, and as they were going, they met a man from Cyrene named Simon, (the father of Alexander and Rufus,) who was coming into the city from the country. They seized him, put the cross on him, and made him carry it behind Jesus.

A large crowd of people followed him; among them were some women who were weeping and wailing for him. Jesus turned to them and said, "Women of Jerusalem! Don't cry for me, but for yourselves and your children.

For the days are coming when people will say, 'How lucky are the women who never had children, who never bore babies, who never nursed them!' That will be the time when people will say to the mountains, 'Fall on us!' and to the hills, 'Hide us!' For if such things as these are done when the wood is green, what will happen when it is dry?"

Two other men, both of them criminals, were also led out to be put to death with Jesus.

> ***INSIGHT:*** *Some manuscripts include: (In this way the scripture came true which says, "He was included with criminals.")*

They took Jesus to a place called Golgotha, which means "The Place of the Skull." There they tried to give him wine mixed with a drug called myrrh, but after tasting it, Jesus would not drink it. There they crucified him and the two criminals, one on his right and the other on his left.

Jesus said, "Forgive them, Father! They don't know what they are doing."

It was nine o'clock in the morning when they crucified him.

Pilate wrote a notice and had it put on the cross. "Jesus of Nazareth, the King of the Jews," is what he wrote. Many people read it, because the place where Jesus was crucified was not far from the city. The notice was written in Hebrew, Latin, and Greek.

The chief priests said to Pilate, "Do not write 'The King of the Jews,' but rather, 'This man said, I am the King of the Jews.'"

Pilate answered, "What I have written stays written."

After the soldiers had crucified Jesus, they took his clothes and divided them into four parts, one part for each soldier. They also took the robe, which was made of one piece of woven cloth, without any seams in it. The soldiers said to one another, "Let's not tear it; let's throw dice to see who will get it." This happened to make the scripture come true:

> "They divided my clothes among themselves, and gambled for my robe." FP Psalm 22:18

And this is what the soldiers did. After that they sat there and watched him.

People passing by shook their heads and hurled insults at Jesus: "Aha! You were going to tear down the Temple and build it back up in three days! Save yourself if you are God's Son! Come on down from the cross!"

In the same way the chief priests and the teachers of the Law and the elders made fun of him. "He saved others; let him save himself if he is the Messiah whom God has chosen! Isn't he the king of Israel? If he will come down off the cross now, we will believe in him! He trusts in God and claims to be God's Son. Well, then, let us see if God wants to save him now!"

The soldiers also made fun of him; they came up to him and offered him cheap wine, and said ,"Save yourself if you are the king of the Jews!"

One of the criminals hanging there hurled insults at him: "Aren't you the Messiah? Save yourself and us!"

The other one, however, rebuked him, saying, "Don't you fear God? You received the same sentence he did. Ours, however, is only right, because we are getting what we deserve for what we did; but he has done no wrong."

And he said to Jesus, "Remember me, Jesus, when you come as King!"

Jesus said to him, "I promise you that today you will be in Paradise with me."

Standing close to Jesus' cross were his mother, his mother's sister, Mary the wife of Clopas, and Mary Magdalene. Jesus saw his mother and the disciple he loved standing there; so he said to his mother, "He is your son."

Then he said to the disciple, "She is your mother."

From that time the disciple took her to live in his home.

INSIGHT: *Crucifixion caused intense suffering. Severe local inflammation produced traumatic fever, which was aggravated by the exposure to the heat of the sun, the strained position of the body and insufferable thirst. The wounds swelled about the rough nails and the torn and lacerated tendons and nerves caused excruciating agony. The arteries of the head and stomach were surcharged with blood and a terrific throbbing headache ensued.*

Tetanus not rarely supervened and the rigors of the attending convulsions would tear at the wounds and add to the burden of the pain, till at last the bodily forces were exhausted and the victim sank to unconsciousness and death. Victims seldom died before thirty-six hours had passed. Jesus died within six hours, thus causing amazement among the people. Quoted from The International Standard Bible Encyclopaedia.

249 Death of Jesus

Matthew 27:45-56; Mark 15:33-41; Luke 23:44-49; John 19:28-30

It was about twelve o'clock when the sun stopped shining and darkness covered the whole country until three o'clock. At three o'clock Jesus cried out with a loud shout, "Eloi, Eloi, lema sabachthani?" which means, "My God, my God, why did you abandon me?"

Some of the people standing there heard him and said, "He is calling for Elijah!" One of them ran up at once, took a sponge, soaked it in cheap wine, put it on the end of a stick, and tried to make him drink it.

But the others said, "Wait, let us see if Elijah is coming to save him!"

Jesus knew that by now everything had been completed; and in order to make the Scripture come true he said,

"I am thirsty." FP Psalm 69:21

A bowl was there, full of cheap wine; so a sponge was soaked in the wine, put on a stalk of hyssop, and lifted up to his lips. Jesus took the wine and said, "It is finished!"

Jesus cried out in a loud voice, "Father! In your hands I place my spirit!" Then he bowed his head and gave up his spirit.

Then the curtain hanging in the Temple was torn in two from top to bottom. The earth shook, the rocks split apart, the graves broke open, and many of God's people who had died were raised to life. They left the graves; and after Jesus rose from death, they went into the Holy City, where many people saw them.

The army officer saw what had happened, and he praised God, saying, "Certainly he was a good man!" When the soldiers with him who were watching Jesus saw the earthquake and everything else that happened, they were terrified and said, "He really was the Son of God!"

When the people who had gathered there to watch the spectacle saw what had happened, they all went back home, beating their breasts in sorrow. All those who knew Jesus personally, including the women who had followed him from Galilee and helped him stood at a distance to watch.

Among them were Mary Magdalene, Mary the mother of the younger James and of Joseph, the wife of Zebedee, and Salome.

250 Jesus' Side Pierced

John 19:31-37

Then the Jewish authorities asked Pilate to allow them to break the legs of the men who had been crucified, and to take the bodies down from the crosses.

They requested this because it was Friday, and they did not want the bodies to stay on the crosses on the Sabbath, since the coming Sabbath was especially holy. So the soldiers went and broke the legs of the first man and then of the other man who had been crucified with Jesus. But when they came to Jesus they saw that he was already dead, so they did not break his legs. One of the soldiers, however, plunged his spear into Jesus' side, and at once blood and water poured out.

INSIGHT: *"...blood and water poured out..." This phenomena could only happen if there was a rupture of the heart as a consequence of supreme mental agony and sorrow. Dr. Walshe, professor of medicine in University College, London, one of the greatest authorities on the disease of the heart, says that a "piercing shriek" is always uttered immediately before the end and death is instantaneous.*

Quoted from The International Standard Bible Encyclopaedia.

(The one who saw this happen has spoken of it, so that you also may believe. What he said is true, and he knows that he speaks the truth.) This was done to make the scripture come true:

"Not one of his bones will be broken." FP Psalm 34:20

And there is another scripture that says,

"People will look at him whom they pierced." FP Zechariah 12:10

251 Burial of Jesus

Matthew 27:57-61; Mark 15:42-47; Luke 23:50-56; John 19:38-42

It was toward evening when Joseph, a rich man from Aramathea, arrived. He was a good and honorable man, a respected member of the Council, who was waiting for the coming of the Kingdom of God.

Although a member of the Council, he had not agreed with their decision and action. (Joseph was a follower of Jesus, but in secret, because he was afraid of the Jewish authorities.)

It was Preparation day (that is, the day before the Sabbath), so Joseph went in boldly into the presence of Pilate and asked him for the body of Jesus. Pilate was surprised to hear that Jesus was already dead.

He called the army officer and asked him if Jesus had been dead a long time. After hearing the officer's report, Pilate told Joseph he could have the body.

Pilate gave orders for the body to be given to Joseph.

Nicodemus, who at first had gone to see Jesus at night, went with Joseph, taking with him about one hundred pounds of spices, a mixture of myrrh and aloes. Joseph bought a linen sheet. The two men took Jesus' body and wrapped it in linen cloths with the spices according to the Jewish custom of preparing a body for burial.

There was a garden in the place where Jesus had been put to death, and in it there was a new tomb which Joseph had just recently dug out of solid rock, where no one had ever been buried.

Since it was the day before the Sabbath and because the tomb was close by, they placed Jesus' body there.

Then Joseph rolled a large stone across the entrance to the tomb and went away.

The women, Mary Magdalene and the other Mary (the mother of Joseph), who had followed Jesus from Galilee went with Joseph and saw the tomb and how Jesus' body was placed in it. Then they went back home and prepared the spices and ointments for the body.

On the Sabbath day they rested, as the Law commanded.

IX. PERIOD OF RESURRECTION

The events during the forty days between Resurrection and Jesus' Ascension cannot be arranged in journeys as Jesus just appeared and disappeared at will. Of the ten recorded appearances, five were on the day of Resurrection, the first on Easter Sunday.

At Jerusalem:

1 Mary Magdalene,
2 the other women
3 Simon Peter
4 ten disciples {Thomas being absent
5 a week later to the eleven disciples
6 then to James, the Lord's brother;
7 Near Emmaus to two disciples, not apostles
8 Near the Sea of Galilee with seven of the apostles
9 On a mountain in Galilee with over 500 of his disciples
10 Near Bethany, 40 days after the resurrection, to the eleven disciples

INSIGHT: *The events during the forty days between the Resurrection and the Ascension cannot be arranged in journeys as Jesus just appeared and disappeared at will. Of the ten recorded appearances, five were on the Day of Resurrection.*

252 Guard at the Grave

Matthew 27:62-66

The next day, which was a Sabbath, the chief priests and the Pharisees met with Pilate and said, "Sir, we remember that while that liar was still alive he said, 'I will be raised to life three days later.'

"Give orders, then, for his tomb to be carefully guarded until the third day, so that his disciples will not be able to go and steal the body, and then tell the people that he was raised from death. This last lie would be even worse than the first one."

"Take a guard," Pilate told them; "go and make the tomb as secure as you can."

So they left and made the tomb secure by putting a seal on the stone and leaving the guard on watch.

253 The Resurrection

Matthew 28:1-15; Mark 16:1-11; Luke 24:1-12; John 20:1-18

After the Sabbath, as Sunday morning was dawning, suddenly there was a violent earthquake; an angel of the Lord came down from heaven, rolled the stone away, and sat on it. His appearance was like lightning, and his clothes were white as snow. The guards were so afraid that they trembled and became like dead men.

Very early on Sunday morning the women (Mary Magdalene, Mary the mother of James, and Salome) went to the tomb, carrying the spices they had prepared. On the way they said to one another, "Who will roll the stone away for us from the entrance to the tomb?" (It was a very large stone.) Then the women looked up and saw that the stone had already been rolled back. So they entered the tomb; but they did not find the body of the Lord Jesus.

They saw a young man sitting at the right, wearing a white robe and they were alarmed.

"Don't be alarmed," he said. "You must not be afraid. I know you are looking for Jesus of Nazareth, who was crucified. He is not here; he has been raised! Look, here is the place where he was placed. Now go and give this message to his disciples, including Peter: 'He is going to Galilee ahead of you; there you will see him, just as he told you.' "

They stood there puzzled about this, when suddenly two men in bright shining clothes stood by them. Full of fear, the women bowed down to the ground, as the men said to them, "Why are you looking among the dead for one who is alive? He is not here; he has been raised. Remember what he said to you while he was in Galilee: 'The Son of Man must be handed over to sinners, be crucified, and three days later rise to life.'"

Then the women remembered his words.

So they went out and ran from the tomb, distressed and terrified, yet filled with joy. They said nothing to anyone.

They went running to Simon Peter and the other disciple whom Jesus loved, and told them, "They have taken the Lord from the tomb, and we don't know where they have put him!"

Then Peter and the other disciple went to the tomb. The two of them were running, but the other disciple ran faster than Peter and reached the tomb first. He bent over and saw the linen cloths, but he did not go in.

Behind him came Simon Peter, and he went straight into the tomb. He saw the linen cloths lying there and the cloth which had been round Jesus' head. It was not lying with the linen cloths but was rolled up by itself.

Then the other disciple, who had reached the tomb first, also went in; he saw and believed. (They still did not understand the scripture which said that he must rise from death.) Then the disciples went back home, amazed at what had happened.

Jesus appeared first to Mary Magdalene, from whom he had driven out seven demons.

Mary stood crying outside the tomb. While she was still crying, she bent over and looked in the tomb and saw two angels there dressed in white, sitting where the body of Jesus had been, one at the head and the other at the feet. "Woman, why are you crying?" they asked her.

She answered, "They have taken my Lord away, and I do not know where they have put him!"

Then she turned around and saw Jesus standing there; but she did not know that it was Jesus. "Woman, why are you crying?" Jesus asked her. "Who is it that you are looking for?"

She thought he was the gardener, so she said to him, "If you took him away, sir, tell me where you have put him, and I will go and get him."

Jesus said to her, "Mary!"

She turned toward him and said in Hebrew, "Rabboni!" (This means "Teacher.")

"Do not hold on to me," Jesus told her, "because I have not yet gone back up to the Father. But go to my brothers and tell them that I am returning to Him who is my Father and their Father, my God and their God."

"So Mary Magdalene went and told the disciples that she had seen the Lord and related to them what he had told her. They were mourning and crying; and when they heard her say that Jesus was alive and that she had seen him, they did not believe her.

Suddenly Jesus met the other women, as they ran to tell his disciples. He said, "Peace be with you." They came up to him, took hold of his feet, and worshiped him. "Do not be afraid," Jesus said to them. "Go and tell my brothers to go to Galilee and there they will see me."

Then the women remembered his words, returned from the tomb, and told all these things to the eleven disciples and all the rest. The women were Joanna, Salome, Mary the mother of James; they and the other women with them told these things to the apostles. But the apostles thought that what the women said was nonsense, and they did not believe them.

While the women went on their way, some of the soldiers guarding the tomb went back to the city and told the chief priests everything that had happened. The chief priests met with the elders and made their plan; they gave a large sum of money to the soldiers and said, "You are to say that his disciples came during the night and stole his body while you were asleep. And if the Governor should hear of this, we will convince him that you are innocent, and you will have nothing to worry about."

The guards took the money and did what they were told to do. And so that is the report spread around by the Jews to this very day.

54 Jesus Appears to Two Disciples and Peter

Mark 16:12-13; Luke 24:13-35

On that same day two of Jesus' followers were going to a village named Emmaus, about seven miles from Jerusalem, and they were talking to each other about all the things that had happened. As they talked and discussed, Jesus himself drew near and walked along with them; they saw him, but somehow did not recognize him. Jesus said to them, "What are you talking about to each other as you walk along?"

They stood still, with sad faces. One of them, named Cleopas, asked him, "Are you the only visitor in Jerusalem who doesn't know the things that have been happening there these last few days?"

"What things?" he asked.

"The things that happened to Jesus of Nazareth," they answered. "This man was a prophet and was considered by God and by all the people to be powerful in everything he said and did. Our chief priests and rulers handed him over to be sentenced to death, and he was crucified. And we had hoped that he would be the one who was going to set Israel free!

"Besides all that, this is now the third day since it happened. Some of the women of our group surprised us; they went at dawn to the tomb; but could not find his body. They came back saying they had seen a vision of angels who told them that he is alive. Some of our group went to the tomb and found it exactly as the women had said, but they did not see him."

Then Jesus said to them, "How foolish you are, how slow you are to believe everything the prophets said! Was it not necessary for the Messiah to suffer these things and then to enter his glory?" And Jesus explained to them what was said about himself in all the Scriptures, beginning with the books of Moses and the writings of all the prophets.

As they came near the village to which they were going, Jesus acted as if he were going farther; but they held him back, saying, "Stay with us; the day is almost over and it is getting dark." So he went in to stay with them.

He sat down to eat with them, took the bread, and said the blessing; then he broke the bread and gave it to them. Then their eyes were opened and they recognized him, but he disappeared from their sight. They said to each other, "Wasn't it like a fire burning in us when he talked to us on the road and explained the Scriptures to us?"

They got up at once and went back to Jerusalem, where they found the eleven disciples gathered together with the others and saying, "The Lord is risen indeed! He has appeared to Simon!"

The two then explained to them what had happened on the road, and how they had recognized the Lord when he broke bread, but these would not believe it.

255 Jesus Appears to Disciples

Luke 24:36-49; John 20:19-29

While the two were telling them this, suddenly the Lord himself stood among them and said to them, "Peace be with you." They were terrified, thinking that they were seeing a ghost. It was late that Sunday evening, and the disciples were gathered together behind locked doors, because they were afraid of the Jewish authorities.

But he said to them, "Why are you alarmed? Why are these doubts coming up in your minds? Look at my hands and my feet and see that it is I myself. Feel me, and you will know, for a ghost doesn't have flesh and bones, as you can see I have."

He said this and showed them his hands and his feet. They still could not believe, they were so full of joy and wonder; so he asked them, "Do you have anything here to eat?" They gave him a piece of cooked fish, which he took and ate in their presence.

Then Jesus said to them again, "Peace be with you. As the Father sent me, so I send you." Then he breathed on them and said, "Receive the Holy Spirit. If you forgive people's sins, they are for-given; if you do not forgive them, they are not forgiven."

Then he said to them, "These are the very things I told you while I was still with you: everything written about me in the Law of Moses, the writings of the prophets, and the Psalms had to come true."

Then he opened their minds to understand the Scriptures, and said to them, "This is what is written: the Messiah must suffer and must rise from death three days later, and in his name the message about repentance and the forgiveness of sins must be preached to all nations, beginning in Jerusalem. You are witness of these things. And I myself will send upon you what my Father has promised. But you must wait in the city until the power from above comes down upon you."

One of the twelve disciples, Thomas (called the Twin), was not with them when Jesus came. So the other disciples told him, "We have seen the Lord."

Thomas said to them, "Unless I see the scars of the nails in his hands and put my finger on those scars and my hand in his side, I will not believe."

A week later the disciples were together again indoors, and Thomas was with them. The doors were locked, but Jesus came and stood among them and said, "Peace be with you." Then he said to Thomas, "Put your finger here, and look at my hands; then reach out your hand and put it in my side. Stop your doubting, and believe!"

Thomas answered him, "My Lord and my God."

Jesus said to him, "Do you believe because you see me? How happy are those who believe without seeing me!"

256 Jesus Appears to Seven Disciples

John 21:1-14

After this, Jesus appeared once more to his disciples at Lake Tiberias (Lake Galilee). This is how it happened. Simon Peter, Thomas (called the Twin), Nathanael (the one from Cana in Galilee), the sons of Zebedee, and two other disciples of Jesus were all together. Simon Peter said to the others, "I am going fishing."

"We will come with you," they told him. So they went out in a boat; but all that night they did not catch a thing. As the sun was rising, Jesus stood at the water's edge, but the disciples did not know that it was Jesus. Then he asked them, "Young men, haven't you caught anything?"

"Not a thing," they answered

He said to them, "Throw your net out on the right side of the boat, and you will catch some."

So they threw the net out and could not pull it back in, because they had caught so many fish. The disciple whom Jesus loved said to Peter, "It is the Lord!" When Peter heard that it was the Lord, he wrapped his outer garment round him (for he had taken his clothes off) and jumped into the water. The other disciples came to shore in the boat, pulling the net full of fish. They were not very far from land, about a hundred yards away. When they stepped ashore, they saw a charcoal fire there with fish on it and some bread. Then Jesus said to them, "Bring some of the fish you have just caught."

Simon Peter went aboard and dragged the net ashore full of big fish, a hundred and fifty-three in all; even though there were so many, still the net did not tear. Jesus said to them, "Come and eat." None of the disciples dared ask him, "Who are you?" because they knew it was the Lord. So Jesus went over, took the bread, and gave it to them; he did the same with the fish.

This, then, was the third time Jesus appeared to the disciples after he was raised from death.

257 Jesus and Peter

John 21:15-19

After they had eaten, Jesus said to Simon Peter, "Simon son of John, do you love me more than these others do?"

"Yes, Lord," he answered, "you know that I love you."

Jesus said to him, "Take care of my lambs." A second time Jesus said to him, "Simon son of John, do you love me?"

"Yes, Lord," he answered, "you know that I love you."

Jesus said to him, "Take care of my sheep." A third time Jesus said, "Simon son of John, do you love me?"

Peter became sad because Jesus asked him the third time, "Do you love me?" and so he said to him, "Lord, you know everything; you know that I love you!"

Jesus said to him, "Take care of my sheep. I am telling you the truth: when you were young, you used to get ready and go anywhere you wanted to; but when you are old, you will stretch out your hands and someone else will tie you up and take you where you don't want to go." (In saying this, Jesus was indicating the way in which Peter would die and bring glory to God.) Then Jesus said to him, "Follow me!"

258 Jesus and the Other Disciple

John 21:20-24

Peter turned around and saw behind him that other disciple, whom Jesus loved - the one who had leaned close to Jesus at the meal and had asked, "Lord, who is going to betray you?" When Peter saw him, he asked Jesus, "Lord, what about this man?"

Jesus answered him, "If I want him to live until I come, what is that to you? Follow me!"

So a report spread among the followers of Jesus that this disciple would not die. But Jesus did not say that he would not die; he said, "If I want him to live until I come, what is that to you?"

He is the disciple who spoke of these things, the one who also wrote them down; and we know that what he said is true.

259 The Great Commission

Matthew 28:16-20; Mark 16:14-18

The eleven disciples went to the hill in Galilee where Jesus had told them to go. When they saw him, they worshiped him, even though some of them doubted. Jesus drew near and said to them, "I have been given all authority in heaven and on earth.

"Go, then, to all peoples everywhere and make them my disciples: baptize them in the name of the Father, the Son, and the Holy Spirit, and teach them to obey everything I have commanded you. And I will be with you always, to the end of the age."

Last of all, Jesus appeared to the eleven disciples as they were eating. He scolded them, because they did not have faith and because they were too stubborn to believe those who had seen him alive. He said to them, "Go throughout the whole world and preach the gospel to all people. Whoever believes and is baptized will be saved; whoever does not believe will be condemned.

"Believers will be given the power to perform miracles: they will drive out demons in my name; they will speak in strange tongues; if they pick up snakes or drink any poison, they will not be harmed; they will place their hands on sick people, and these will get well."

260 Jesus Ascends to Heaven

Mark 16:19-20; Luke 24:50-53

Then he led them out of the city as far as Bethany, where he raised his hands and blessed them. As he was blessing them, he departed from them and was taken up into heaven and sat at the right side of God. They worshiped him and went back into Jerusalem, filled with great joy, and spent all their time in the Temple giving thanks to God. The disciples went and preached everywhere, and the Lord worked with them and proved that their preaching was true by the miracles that were performed.

261 Purpose of John's Book and Conclusions

John 20:30-31, 21:25

In his disciples' presence Jesus performed many other miracles which are not written down in this book. But these have been written in order that you may believe that Jesus is the Messiah, the Son of God, and that through your faith in him you may have life.

Now, there are many other things that Jesus did. If they were all written down one by one, I suppose that the whole world could not hold the books that would be written.

262 BIBLICAL INSIGHTS

Acts 1:1-12

Dear Theophilus:

In my first book [Luke] I wrote about all the things that Jesus did and taught from the time he began his work until the day he was taken up to heaven. Before he was taken up, he gave instructions by the power of the Holy Spirit to the men he had chosen as his apostles.

For forty days after his death he appeared to them many times in ways that proved beyond doubt that he was alive. They saw him, and he talked with them

about the Kingdom of God. And when they came together, he gave them this order: "Do not leave Jerusalem, but wait for the gift I told you about, the gift my Father promised. John baptized with water, but in a few days you will be baptized with the Holy Spirit."

When the apostles met together with Jesus, they asked him, "Lord, will you at this time give the Kingdom back to Israel?"

Jesus said to them, "The times and occasions are set by my Father's own authority, and it is not for you to know when they will be. But when the Holy Spirit comes upon you, you will be filled with power, and you will be witnesses for me in Jerusalem, in all of Judea and Samaria, and to the ends of the earth." After saying this, he was taken up to heaven as they watched him, and a cloud hid him from their sight.

They still had their eyes fixed on the sky as he went away, when two men dressed in white suddenly stood beside them and said, "Galileans, why are you standing there looking up at the sky? This Jesus, who was taken from you into heaven, will come back in the same way that you saw him go to heaven."

Then the apostles went back to Jerusalem from the Mount of Olives, which is about half a mile from the city

263 BIBLICAL INSIGHTS

I Corinthians 15:6-7

Then he appeared to more than five hundred of his followers at once, most of whom are still alive, although some have died. Then he appeared to James, and then to all the apostles.

X. GOD'S PLAN FOR YOUR LIFE

ETERNAL LIFE

God loves you and wants you to experience His peace and life.

The Bible says:

"For God loved the world so much that he gave his only Son, that everyone who believes in him may not die but have eternal life. For God did not send his son into the world to be its judge, but to be its saviors." John 3:16, 17

UNION WITH GOD--NOT SEPARATION

By nature man is separated from God.

The Bible says:

"...everyone has sinned and is far away from God's saving presence." Romans 3:23

GOD'S REMEDY IS THE CROSS

God's love bridges the gap of separation between God and you. Jesus paid the penalty for your sins when He died on the cross and rose from the grave.

The Bible says:

"Christ himself carried our sins in his body to the cross." Peter 2:24

MAN'S RESPONSE IS TO RECEIVE CHRIST

You cross the gap into God's family when you receive Christ as your personal Savior.

The Bible says:

"Some, however, did receive him and believed in him; so he gave them the right to become God's children." John 1:12

PRAYER OF COMMITMENT

You can receive Christ right now by faith through prayer. God knows your heart and is not so concerned with your words as He is with your attitude. Prayer is talking with God. A sample prayer follows. If this prayer expresses the desire in your heart, then you can use it as your prayer right now:

"Lord Jesus, I know I am a sinner. I need you. I believe you died for my sins. Right now, I turn from my sins and open the door of my life and receive You as my Savior and Lord.

Thank you for forgiving my sins and giving me eternal life. I give you control of my life. Make me the kind of person You want me to be. Amen."

WHERE DO I GO FROM HERE?

If you have prayed this prayer, we would love to hear from you.
If you have questions, please contact us at the following email address.
Email: pmdyck@gmail.com

You need to begin to grow in your relationship with Christ. You do this by talking to Him. Pray about everything. Pray specifically and pray honestly. God talks to you through the Bible; it is your spiritual food. Read it daily. Without spiritual food, you will become weak and sickly in your spiritual life.

Share your new life with other people. This is witnessing. This comes about as a natural result of growing spiritually.

Finally, find other believers who can help you and with whom you can fellowship. If possible, attend a Bible study class where you can ask questions and continue to grow into spiritual maturity.

SOME SCRIPTURES TO HELP YOU:

WHEN AFFLICTED:

Psalm 119:67, 71, 75 -- often providential
Psalm 34:19 -- God will deliver

WHEN ANXIOUS:

Philippians 4:6, 7 -- relieved through prayer
I Peter 5:7 -- God cares for you

WHEN DISCOURAGED:

Galatians 6:9 -- don't give up
Isaiah 41:10 -- God will strengthen and help

WHEN DOUBTING:

John 3:16 -- eternal life promised
I John 5:11-13 -- you can be sure

WHEN LONELY:

Hebrews 13:5, 6 -- His presence promised
Psalm 16:11 -- joy in His presence

WHEN WORRIED:

Philippians 4:19 -- God will provide
I John 5:14, 15 -- claim His promises
Hebrews 13:5, 6 -- will never forsake you

76738742R00102

Made in the USA
Columbia, SC
09 September 2017